Born in São Paulo, Brazil, **Betty Milan** is the author of novels, essays, and plays that have been published in Brazil, France, Spain, Portugal, Argentina, and China. Before turning to writing, she earned her medical degree at the University of São Paulo and trained in psychoanalysis with Jacques Lacan in France, where she served as his assistant at the Department of Psychoanalysis, University of Paris 8.

Mari Ruti was Distinguished Professor of Critical Theory at the University of Toronto. She was the author of thirteen books, including *Between Levinas and Lacan: Self, Other, Ethics* (2015) and *Distillations: Theory, Ethics, Affect* (2018), both published with Bloomsbury.

Clifford E. Landers has translated from Portuguese almost forty novels and more than one hundred shorter works of fiction. A professor emeritus at New Jersey City University, he lives with his wife Vasda Bonafini Landers in Naples, Florida.

Chris Vanderwees is a psychoanalyst, registered psychotherapist, and clinical supervisor at St. John the Compassionate Mission in Toronto, Canada. He is the author of *Speaking of Lacan* and the co-author of *Psychoanalysis and the New Rhetoric*. He is an affiliate of the Toronto Psychoanalytic Society and a member of the Lacanian School of Psychoanalysis.

T0270000

Psychoanalytic Horizons

Psychoanalysis is unique in being at once a theory and a therapy, a method of critical thinking and a form of clinical practice. Now in its second century, this fusion of science and humanism derived from Freud has outlived all predictions of its demise. **Psychoanalytic Horizons** evokes the idea of a convergence between realms as well as the outer limits of a vision. Books in the series test disciplinary boundaries and will appeal to scholars and therapists who are passionate not only about the theory of literature, culture, media, and philosophy but also, above all, about the real life of ideas in the world.

Series Editors
Esther Rashkin, Mari Ruti, and Peter L. Rudnytsky

Advisory Board
Salman Akhtar, Doris Brothers, Aleksandar Dimitrijevic, Lewis Kirshner, Humphrey Morris, Hilary Neroni, Dany Nobus, Lois Oppenheim, Donna Orange, Peter Redman, Laura Salisbury, Alenka Zupančič

Volumes in the Series:
Mourning Freud
by Madelon Sprengnether
Does the Internet Have an Unconscious?: Slavoj Žižek and Digital Culture
by Clint Burnham
In the Event of Laughter: Psychoanalysis, Literature and Comedy
by Alfie Bown
On Dangerous Ground: Freud's Visual Cultures of the Unconscious
by Diane O'Donoghue
For Want of Ambiguity: Order and Chaos in Art, Psychoanalysis, and Neuroscience
by Ludovica Lumer and Lois Oppenheim
Life Itself Is an Art: The Life and Work of Erich Fromm
by Rainer Funk

Born After: Reckoning with the German Past
by Angelika Bammer
Critical Theory Between Klein and Lacan: A Dialogue
by Amy Allen and Mari Ruti
Transferences: The Aesthetics and Poetics of the Therapeutic Relationship
by Maren Scheurer
At the Risk of Thinking: An Intellectual Biography of Julia Kristeva
by Alice Jardine, edited by Mari Ruti
The Writing Cure
by Emma Lieber
The Analyst's Desire: The Ethical Foundation of Clinical Practice
by Mitchell Wilson
Our Two-Track Minds: Rehabilitating Freud on Culture
by Robert A. Paul
Norman N. Holland: The Dean of American Psychoanalytic Literary Critics
by Jeffrey Berman
Psychological Roots of the Climate Crisis: Neoliberal Exceptionalism and the Culture of Uncare
by Sally Weintrobe
Circumcision on the Couch: The Cultural, Psychological and Gendered Dimensions of the World's Oldest Surgery
by Jordan Osserman
The Racist Fantasy: Unconscious Roots of Hatred
by Todd McGowan
Antisemitism and Racism: Ethical Challenges for Psychoanalysis
by Stephen Frosh
The Ethics of Immediacy: Dangerous Experience in Freud, Woolf, and Merleau-Ponty
by Jeffrey McCurry
Analyzed by Lacan: A Personal Account
by Betty Milan

ANALYZED BY LACAN

A Personal Account

Betty Milan

Translations by
Clifford E. Landers and Chris Vanderwees

BLOOMSBURY ACADEMIC
NEW YORK • LONDON • OXFORD • NEW DELHI • SYDNEY

BLOOMSBURY ACADEMIC
Bloomsbury Publishing Inc
1385 Broadway, New York, NY 10018, USA
50 Bedford Square, London, WC1B 3DP, UK
29 Earlsfort Terrace, Dublin 2, Ireland

BLOOMSBURY, BLOOMSBURY ACADEMIC and the Diana logo are trademarks of
Bloomsbury Publishing Plc

Cover design by Daniel Benneworth-Gray

Library of Congress Cataloging-in-Publication Data
Names: Milan, Betty, author. | Vanderwees, Chris, translator. | Landers, Clifford E.,
translator. | Milan, Betty. Lacan ainda. English. | Milan, Betty. Adeus, doutor. English.
Title: Analyzed by Lacan : a personal account / Betty Milan ; translations
by Chris Vanderwees and Clifford E. Landers.
Description: New York : Bloomsbury Academic, [2024] |
Series: Psychoanalytic horizons | Includes bibliographical references. |
Summary: "The first English translation of Betty Milan's firsthand
testimony as Jacques Lacan's patient and later assistant, as well as the
play, since adapted into a film, that was inspired by this experience"–Provided by
publisher. Identifiers: LCCN 2023015198 (print) | LCCN 2023015199 (ebook) | ISBN
9798765106198 (paperback) | ISBN 9798765106204 (hardback) | ISBN 9798765106228
(pdf) | ISBN 9798765106211 (epub) | ISBN 9798765106235 (ebook other)
Subjects: LCSH: Milan, Betty–Mental health. | Authors, Brazilian–20th century–Biography.
| Lacan, Jacques, 1901–1981. | LCGFT: Autobiographies. | Drama.
Classification: LCC PQ9698.23.I347 Z46 2024 (print) | LCC PQ9698.23.I347
(ebook) | DDC 869.8/4203 [B]–dc23/eng/20230624
LC record available at https://lccn.loc.gov/2023015198
LC ebook record available at https://lccn.loc.gov/2023015199

ISBN: HB: 979-8-7651-0620-4
           PB: 979-8-7651-0619-8
           ePDF: 979-8-7651-0622-8
           eBook: 979-8-7651-0621-1

Series: Psychoanalytic Horizons

Typeset by Integra Software Services Pvt. Ltd.
Printed and bound in Great Britain

To find out more about our authors and books visit www.bloomsbury.com
and sign up for our newsletters.

CONTENTS

PREFACE

Translated by Chris Vanderwees

Lacan has been with me since 1971, when I met him. He has been with me for more than four decades. How can I explain this constant companionship? Lacan offered me an encounter with myself that never ceased to be renewed—an effect produced by his way of conducting an analysis.

His theory has spread through the publication and translation of the *Seminars*, but his clinical practice is much less well known for reasons that I explain in this book. I wrote *Why Lacan*—the memoir that is the first chapter of this book—to shed light on this. I wanted to show what his scope was and to dispel damaging rumors, such as the one that he shortened the analytic session to earn more money.

A lot of water went under the bridge before I was ready to write my memoir. Between 1973 and 1977, I underwent an analysis with Lacan that, initially, I had not even considered undertaking. I explain in this book how the Doctor genuinely captivated me and how I left Brazil behind to make my home in France. It was not out of courage that I left my native country and lived in another language; it was because I had no other choice. Lacan, who knew a lot about theater, told me at the time that I had left Brazil in order to discover America. In a certain sense, this is what happened, thanks to an analysis where the analysand's journey was a traversal of her "subjective epic."

The reference to theater is as present in Freud's *oeuvre* as in Lacan's approach. For the founder of psychoanalysis, we all share something with tragic heroes, like Oedipus, like Hamlet, because the unconscious acts and speaks in our place, and we live its returns with a guilty conscience. Following Freud, Lacan gave psychoanalytic treatment the magnitude of an epic. He relied on the resources of the theater both in his seminars and in his practice as a clinician.

Since my analysis, several publishers have solicited my memoir. In the 1990s, responding positively to them was beyond my capacity, but I wrote a novel based on my analysis, whose central themes were immigration, xenophobia, and the importance of the mother tongue. It seemed to me that the best way to dig inside myself about what had happened in the analysis was through the path of literature. Theoretical discourse could have locked me in jargon and prevented me from deepening the subjective questions that were at work in me.

Ten years later, still inspired by my analysis, I wrote a play staged in 2009 at the Théâtre du Rond-Point in Paris. This play is, above all, about the theme of motherhood. Like her ancestors, the heroine of Lebanese origin must produce a male firstborn to accomplish what her family expects of her. Pregnancy therefore becomes the problem of her life: after two miscarriages, her husband leaves her. Is motherhood inaccessible to her? Can she not identify with the other women in her family? Or is there another reason? Thanks to the analysis with the Doctor, the heroine can accept her body, recognize her female sexuality, and become a mother. The play demonstrates that gender troubles can have unconscious reasons.

After its presentation in France, I wanted my play to be translated into English. It was read at the New School in 2018 at the invitation of Paola Mieli. Richard Ledes, who moderated the lecture, told me that he wanted to make a film adaptation of it. I signed the rights over to him in 2020. It would become the first film featuring Lacan.

The gods were with us and the film was made the following year in 2021. I then gathered my courage to write *Why Lacan* as a testament to the relevance of the Doctor's work.

Lacan made extensive use of the so-called short session. In fact, the time of the session was variable. Lacan was not guided by the time of Kronos, the time that passes, but that of Kairos, the moment of opportunity that we seize. What counted for him was the discourse of the analysand, not the clock. As soon as the essential was said, the session was over, and the analyst had fulfilled his role. In his own way, Lacan taught us not to waste time.

Lacan did not interpret the analysand's discourse by attributing a meaning to it. He interrupted the session and allowed the analysand to interpret the reason for the cut. The analysis continued outside the session. This new way of working was due to a clinical discovery: Lacan had realized that the traditional manner of interpreting could provoke resistance. He therefore changed his practice. From his point of view, psychoanalysis needed to be reinvented.

Why Lacan was written to illustrate this reinvention and also to render Lacan's approach intelligible to the uninitiated.

WHY LACAN
(A Memoir)

Translated by Chris Vanderwees

to the memory of Jacques Lacan

PRELIMINARIES

I did my analysis with Lacan in the 1970s. At the time, a French publisher asked me to write on this subject. The *on* bothered me; I did not follow up. The transference was too great; I did not have enough distance to be able to deliver my testimony. This is why I wrote a novel inspired by my analysis instead. Forty years later, I wanted to come back to what had happened at 5, rue de Lille, where, among other things, I had learned to privilege the opportune moment.

If my work with Lacan did not definitively deliver me from anguish, it changed my life. He allowed me to accept my origins, my biological sex, and motherhood, thanks, on the one hand, to his interest, whose intensity I perceived, and, on the other hand, to his way of working, which is controversial even today. It is this precise point that I want to emphasize from my experience with him. But first, I would like to mention a very significant example. Recently, in a circle of intellectuals, someone expressed his indignation about a session experienced by one of his acquaintances who had undergone an analysis with Lacan in the 1960s. On the couch, the person concerned had spontaneously switched from French to Portuguese, without Lacan's intervention. He had let the analysand speak for a good while without understanding what he was saying, then he had stood up and interrupted the session with a "see you next time." Since nothing that was said could be interpreted, we have to conclude that, for Lacan, the signified of the analysand's discourse had counted less than the passage from one language to another.

For those who know the importance of language for Lacan—he often spoke of the "treasure trove of signifiers"—this is not surprising. So, what was the point of the session? Lacan's silence, followed by an abrupt interruption, highlighted the analysand's desire to speak in his mother tongue, thus giving meaning to the idea that "desire is the desire for recognition." By doing so, the Doctor was at the same time underlining the irreplaceable character of the mother tongue.

It was around this question of language that my analysis took place between 1973 and 1977. Intellectual life in Paris was then in full swing, around Michel Foucault, Michel Serres, Gilles Deleuze, Jacques Derrida, and Julia Kristeva, among others. Lacan was holding his seminar in the large amphitheater of the Faculty of Law, on the Place du Panthéon, where the first to arrive warmed up the place for the others. In the front row sat the familiar and closest disciples of the master, who only entered when the theater was full. In the winter, he wore a black mink coat where the light played, as in his white hair, to which he paid particular attention. Lacan's entrance was a veritable apparition: a silence was gradually established. The master was going to speak, every word was going to be drunk, even when his speech was deprived of intelligibility. Indeed, Lacan was little concerned with being immediately intelligible. He emphasized *Nachträglich*, the Freudian concept translated into French as *après-coup*. *Nachträglich* means that certain facts can only be understood after they have occurred—and Lacan's practice was based on this notion, both in his seminar and in his clinic.

The seminar was addressed to psychoanalysts and intellectuals interested in analytic theory—those who could wait for knowledge. This is why the accusations of elitism directed at Lacan during the last few decades have been misguided. How could a master whose practice demanded the greatest patience submit to the imperatives of immediate communication in his teaching? Lacan taught in his own way, differently from that advocated by professors and communicators, whose transmission is necessarily limpid insofar as it aims to express knowledge already constituted. For Lacan, *non-knowledge* was as important as knowledge, and he gave himself up in public to the discovery of his distinctive path. This is what he did in all his seminars from 1953 to 1980, as if to evoke Antonio Machado: "you make your own path as you walk. As you walk, you make your own road,/and when you look back/you see the path/you will never travel again./Traveler, there is no road;/only a ship's wake on the sea."[1]

Nachträglich was also the basis of the Doctor's practice. He would interrupt the session without explanation, trusting the analysand to discover the reason for the interruption on his or her own. He encouraged the other to analyze themselves. "Go and come back and tell me what you have discovered. Go and decipher the enigma of your

---

1. *Al andar se hace camino / Y al volver la vista atrás / Se ve la senda que nunca / Se ha de volver a pisar / Caminante no hay camino sino estelas en la mar.*

own story." This explains the substitution of the word *patient* for that of *analysand*. The patient's position is that of one who waits for the doctor's wisdom. The analysand's position is that of the person doing the analysis.

In this context, the treatment depends as much on the analysand as on the analyst and the session does not exist without the street. In my case, the session included traveling from 5, rue de Lille to rue de la Harpe, or to use my slip of the tongue, from the Lacan Quarter to the Latin Quarter. On the way, I would ruminate on what had been said and often make a discovery that confirmed the importance of the work. This eureka increased my self-esteem, and the desire for a new session naturally arose.

Lacan maintained that transference thanks to the cut was an effective means of passing on the power to analyze, i.e., his own power, to his analysand. In other words, he invited the analysand to access knowledge of herself. The cut avoids the resistance to analysis that the interpretation of the analysand's discourse by the analyst can provoke. This is due to the fact that discourse has several possible meanings and that the analysand may not recognize herself at all in the one attributed to her by the analyst whose intervention may, in this case, generate a power struggle.

As the interruption of the session took place according to the discourse and not the time of the clock, it was not possible to respect the rule of forty-five minutes per session established by the International Psychoanalytic Association (IPA). For Lacan, as soon as what was essential had been said, the session was over, the analyst had fulfilled his or her role. This is the main reason why the IPA asked him to resign in 1953. He was banned for "deviant practice."

In the same year, to justify the interruption of the session, he wrote "The Function and Field of Speech and Language in Psychoanalysis." One of his analysands was talking non-stop about Dostoyevsky's art, wasting the session's time in endless comments. Lacan interrupted his speech and, in the following session, a fantasy of anal pregnancy arose … a pregnancy that ended in a caesarean section. The interruption had the effect of suspending a fallacious discourse and giving birth to a full speech.

Lacan wanted the analysis to take place without tactics of delay. He condemned wastefulness and that is why he refused to work according to chronological time, thereby allowing the analyst, as well as the analysand, to do what was unexpected. It was not the linear time of

Kronos that guided him, but the time of Kairos, that of the fleeting moment when an opportunity arises that one must know how to seize.

By taking the path of Kairos, Lacan turned psychoanalysis upside down and restored the vitality of its beginnings. What counted was not the analyst's punctuality, but his readiness. In other words, it was not enough to have been trained and to be recognized by one's peers. The analyst had to prove his competence in each session.

The reversal was so significant that the IPA asked Lacan to resign. His teaching was the object of an unusual censorship that made him an outcast. This was a situation that he compared to the "major excommunication" of which Spinoza had been a victim in the seventeenth century.

In 1981, when Lacan died, I chose as an epigraph for his obituary— written for a newspaper in Brazil—a line from Saint-John Perse: "They called me the dark and I lived in brightness." Lacan lit up my path, allowing a descendant of Lebanese immigrants, a victim of the xenophobia of others and of her own, to finally accept herself.

I do not remember everything that happened during the analysis. But what was decisive, I have not forgotten. I have even kept an almost photographic memory of certain facts, such as the image of the Doctor standing at the entrance to the waiting room, in the doorframe, to call in the next analysand. His look went from one to the other, hesitated for a moment, and then he pointed to the chosen one with a wave of his hand before turning on his heels and returning to his office.

More than one analysand has spoken about the impact of Lacan's sessions without questioning the reason for it, either because the transference had not yet been worked through or because it was difficult to shift from the position of the analysand—who is content to associate freely and lets the analyst interpret—to the position of the interpreter. This passage also implies the revelation of facts which the analysand does not always have the desire to divulge. Much of what is said in analysis is stated because the analyst agrees not to reveal anything. I still remember the session where, to tear me out of my silence, Lacan assured me: "Nothing you say will leave here."

If the analyst cannot speak of what he has heard from his patient, except at the cost of becoming a traitor, the patient has the freedom to testify. But often those who become analysts shy away from writing a memoir of their experience of being analyzed in order not to strip themselves of the aura of mystery that, in their imagination, they must preserve in order to exercise their magisterium. However, the fact remains that testimony is important for the transmission of the practice, which is perpetuated in spite of all the detractors of psychoanalysis and the continuous oppositions between analysts.

I worked steadily with Lacan from 1973 to 1977. But it is only now that I wonder how he made an analysis at the limits of the possible into a reality. I say this because at the time I had little fluency in French and deep down I did not really want to engage in an analysis—as is often the case. If I had not had to leave the Brazilian Society of Psychoanalysis (SBP) for irreverence, along with other members deemed undesirable, it is likely that I would never have come to France. My deepest wish was to be recognized as a psychoanalyst abroad so that I could then practice in Brazil. At eighteen, when I entered the Faculty of Medicine at the University of São Paulo, I was already interested in psychoanalysis. As soon as I could, I locked myself in the library to read Freud.

I identified with Lacan because he opposed the IPA. But the fact that the Doctor was French was very important for an unconscious reason, which I will return to in detail, and for the admiration that at the time Brazilian intellectuals had for their counterparts in the country of Descartes.

This aura of France in Brazil had deep roots.[2] There is Jean de Léry's *History of a Voyage to the Land of Brazil* about his experience with the

2. The relationship between Brazil and France dates back to the sixteenth century. Brazil was the object of the covetousness of Nicolas Durand de Villegaignon (1510–72), who settled in Guanabara Bay and founded the Antarctic France in 1555. This was later wiped off the map by the Portuguese. From then on, the country became a literary and philosophical subject for the French.

Jean de Léry, who visited Antarctic France, published *History of a Voyage to the Land of Brazil* in 1578, a small masterpiece about his experience with the anthropophagous indigenous people. The author accuses the French of being more barbaric than cannibals, evoking the massacre of Protestants in Paris on August 24, 1572, during the Night of St. Bartholomew.

After having met three Tupinamba people in Rouen in 1562, Montaigne wrote *Of Cannibals*, where he asserts that Europeans who torture their prisoners before killing them are crueler than indigenous people. The comparison between the Portuguese and the indigenous led Montaigne to criticize European ethnocentrism and to oppose the idea that indigenous people were barbaric. This is also the reason that he is still a reference for Brazilian intellectuals.

indigenous anthropophagi; the famous chapter of Montaigne's *Essays*, "The Cannibals," resulting from his meeting in Rouen with three Tupinambas; the influence of the Enlightenment on the separatists of the Minas Gerais Conspiracy; the French mission sent by Louis XVIII to Brazil, of which the painter Jean-Baptiste Debret left unforgettable testimonies; the teachings of Claude Lévi-Strauss and Fernand Braudel at the University of São Paulo; Michel Foucault's stays in Rio and São Paulo. The numerous literary and cultural exchanges between Brazil and France contributed to my fascination with France.

I heard about Lacan in São Paulo in 1968, at a meeting of intellectuals. There was a French psychoanalyst there who did not want to deal with the May events and spoke only about Lacan. For him, modernity did not reside in the Parisian demonstrations, but rather at 5, rue de Lille. I left the meeting with the same conviction, determined to explore the relationship between psychoanalysis and linguistics and the nature of the *subject of the signifier*, so important in Lacanian theory.

In the eighteenth century, the ideas of the Enlightenment carried by young people trained in Europe influenced the conspirators of Minas Gerais (*inconfidentes mineiros*) who revolted against Portugal and claimed independence. It was no longer possible to pay the taxes demanded by the Portuguese crown, which threatened to use arms to collect them.

In the nineteenth century, during the reign of Don João VI in Brazil, Louis XVIII sent a French mission to Rio that established a system of higher academic education and played an important role in the cultural formation of the country. In addition to his numerous watercolors depicting daily life, the painter Jean-Baptiste Debret (1768–1848), also wrote *A Picturesque and Historic Voyage to Brazil*, which remains a reference.

In the twentieth century, France's presence continued with a second decisive mission, composed of young professors—including Claude Lévi-Strauss and Fernand Braudel—who founded the University of São Paulo in the 1930s. After the Second World War, an intensive program of exchanges between the two countries began. In the 1960s, sociologist Fernando Henrique Cardoso—who would become president of the Republic from 1995 to 2002—was invited to teach at the Sorbonne. The University of São Paulo received philosophers, historians, and anthropologists who became famous. Among them was Michel Foucault, who was officially invited to Brazil five times between 1965 and 1976.

With a few others, we formed a group to decipher the *Écrits*, an objective we only achieved with great difficulty, believing that the difficulty arose from the French language, when in reality it arose from the specificity of Lacan's language. In this respect, we can compare him to James Joyce who, unable to write in Gaelic—a language spoken by a minority—invented his own language in English. This language can be heard every year on Bloomsday, the day of June 16, when the people of Dublin celebrate *Ulysses*, evoking in the streets, theaters, and bars episodes from the life of Leopold Bloom, its main protagonist.

Like Joyce, Lacan invented his language and introduced a new concept, *lalangue*, which concerns the idiosyncratic language of each person. Often only writers are aware of this peculiar form of language. In his own way, the master was a poet, and the link he saw between psychoanalysis and poetry became evident when, during one of his seminars in 1977, he declared that he was not enough of a poet to be a great analyst.[3]

I was already a psychiatrist, but I wanted to get a doctorate in psychiatry, writing a thesis on eclampsia. I was also undergoing analytic training. My deepest wish was to be recognized as a psychoanalyst abroad, so that I could then practice in Brazil. After a psychiatric internship in Brazil, I obtained, through a colleague, Lacan's address in Paris. Despite the military dictatorship in Brazil, the arrests, and the torture, I did not consider doing an analysis abroad. Like many other Brazilians, I was very attached to my country. I wanted to talk to Lacan with the sole purpose of asking him to indicate an analyst who could work with our group in São Paulo to organize a seminar there and to teach his theory. This seemed like a typical request from a person coming from a city where nothing has ever seemed impossible, including bringing the sea from the coast to São Paulo, as the Paulists (the inhabitants of São Paulo) had imagined at the height of their splendor ...

At the time, the great novelty in my field of work was the transformation of the psychiatric asylum into a therapeutic community, and I had met its designer, Maxwell Jones, in São Paulo. We corresponded briefly, and in 1971 I arranged to visit the community he had started in Melrose, Scotland. I had the intention of going to France afterward and perhaps meeting Lacan. I say *perhaps* because no

---

3. I heard Lacan mention this in one of his seminars in 1977.

meeting having been fixed, I could not presume that a person of such notoriety would agree to receive me without an introduction from someone he knew.

From Melrose, I went to Paris where I settled in a hotel on rue des Écoles. I called several times the number that a psychiatrist in São Paulo had given me, but always got the same answer: *there are no Doctors here.* My companion at the time, also a psychiatrist, suggested that we go directly to 5, rue de Lille.

On the door of the building, no sign. We had to wait until someone came out and could inform us. It was a woman, completely absorbed in her thoughts. Perhaps she had just finished a session.

"Could you please tell me Lacan's floor?"
"What? I didn't understand …"
"Lacan … the Doctor's office?"
"It's on the first."

And without a word, she turned her head and continued down the street. We went upstairs and, with my heart pounding, I dared to ring the bell.

The Doctor's secretary, the eternal Gloria, opened the door and said hello to us with her slight foreign accent.

"We couldn't make an appointment before coming …"
"What do you mean?"
"The phone number they gave me in Brazil must be wrong."
"In Brazil?"

Gloria widened her eyes, smiled, and, without asking anything else, led us to the waiting room. Lacan appeared at the door and, welcoming us with a gesture, beckoned us in.

Before making my request for an analyst in São Paulo who could teach a seminar on Lacan's theory, I explained that we had not made an appointment because we had the wrong phone number.

"If the phone did not work, why didn't you come here right away?"

I was puzzled by the question. How could I push open his door without prior authorization? From the outset, the Doctor suggested that I could—and why not?—act on my impulse. He valued the desire, and not the imaginary, of the young stranger, who counted for so little in her own eyes. With a sentence, with a smile, I was won over. He then wanted to know where we were from.

"From São Paulo."

"From Brazil!" exclaimed Lacan emphatically.

This emphasis on our origin revealed the Doctor's interest. He made use of a theatrical resource as he would on other occasions. Since it was I who had answered— my companion remained silent—it was to me that he addressed himself.

"Your ancestors are also Brazilian?"

"My grandparents are Lebanese ... on the side of my mother and my father ... immigrants."

"Interesting ... When did they arrive in Brazil?"

"At the end of the nineteenth century, to escape the war ... and then at the beginning of the twentieth century."

"And you, my dear, what are you doing?"

"I am a psychiatrist. I did an analysis and now I study ... Lacan."

"Really?"

"We have a group in São Paulo that has undertaken to read your *Écrits*. Despite the difficulty, because of the language, we got through the first text, 'The Purloined Letter.' We now want to invite a French analyst recommended by you ... I have a letter from my colleagues here."

I gave him the letter, which he put on his desk after looking at it.

"Very well. Come back tomorrow and you will tell me about the conditions of this invitation."

Then he got up and walked us to the door.

When I left his office, I was no longer the same. By bringing me to talk about my origins, Lacan had sent me back to the history hidden by my ancestors. For them, the integration of the descendants depended on forgetting the past. The Doctor's interest led me to speak about what I had been trying to hide since adolescence: the truth about my origins. He allowed me to be the granddaughter of immigrants. In other words, I left Lacan's office without the shame regarding who I was that I had carried for a long time. All I wanted to do was to return to 5, rue de Lille. This had not escaped the Doctor, whose desire to analyze never wavered.

It is not by chance that he insisted so much on the importance of the *desire of the analyst* in the effectiveness of the cure. He also drew attention to the opposite idea of the *resistance of the analyst*, when at the time we were only talking about the *resistance of the patient*—to whom all and any difficulty in the process was attributed.

I came back the next day with my companion, who was really my shield. As no one is accompanied to see their analyst, his presence attested that my visit was only due to the initiative of my colleagues in São Paulo. But this time, when he appeared at the door, it was me that Lacan looked at and said:

"*Come on in*, my dear."

Come on in, and I entered, determined to talk about the conditions of the invitation.

"The analyst appointed by you would teach your theory in a seminar
   we are organizing."
"Hmm …"
"There will be no cost to him since the participants will pay for it."
"Good, put it all in writing and return tomorrow."

With the *return tomorrow*, he inserted me into the rhythm of analytic work, whose path I secretly wished to follow. He relied on the imperative—*return*—and the regularity of the meetings to open the way to the analysis. Lacan always privileged two resources: the word and time. Hence the importance of the texts "Function and Field of Speech" and "Logical Time" in the *Écrits*.

So I went a third and last time to 5, rue de Lille. But this time it was to tell the Doctor that I wanted to do an analysis with him. Retrospectively, I recognize that what happened there, in 1971, corresponds to the first stage of my analysis, the so-called *preliminary stage*.

Alleging the need to finish a doctoral thesis in Brazil, I pledged to return to Paris within two years and to stay there for four months. The two-year period may have seemed long, but what mattered was the promised word. Lacan said goodbye to me and added, "Above all, don't forget to write to me."

Not only did he express the desire not to lose sight of me, but he also gave me the freedom to return whenever I wished. In other words, *your time will be mine*, which reminds me of the troubadour who called his lady his *suzerain* and himself her *servant*. Could I, who came from such a deeply machismo country, commit myself fully to this new perspective?

It was only much later that I understood Lacan's way of proceeding in the first stage of the analysis. The Doctor took into account the explicit request (*demande*)—to recommend to me an analyst who could go to Brazil—so that my unconscious desire could emerge. He treated my request as the manifest content of a dream, the signified of which must be discovered through the associations of the dreamer.

Of course, he did this because he wanted me to become his analysand. A desire he expressed by *why didn't you come here right away?*, by *return tomorrow*, and *above all*, by *do not forget to write to me*. He made it clear that my engagement in analysis with him was something important. This is how my idea of crossing the ocean again to work with Lacan came to fruition.

The analysis began with three short sessions: twenty minutes for the first and less than ten for the following ones. This was a very short duration for what represented a major turning point, because it was not chronological time that counted, but a *modus operandi* based on deep empathy and the quality of listening. The clock counted as little as the length of a poem in poetry. It took no more than a line for Camões to define the nature of the feeling of love, which is "a discontented contentment" (*contentamento descontente*), or "a pain that hurts, but is not felt" (*dor que dói e não sente*). With a single verse, "we are dust, but loving dust" (*somos pó, mas pó amoroso*), Quevedo showed how life is inseparable from death.

Like the poets, Lacan drew on the treasure trove of language to do much with little. One example is the neologism he coined to evoke the transformation of love into hate (*amour en haine*): *hainamoration*. A single word—which could serve as a subtitle for Shakespeare's *Othello*—to designate the ordinary substitution of hate for love, as if love and hate were two sides of the same coin.

My companion and I returned to Brazil, where I wrote my doctoral thesis in psychiatry on eclampsia, a rare pathology in developed countries, but then very widespread in Brazil, due to the lack of resources in the prenatal field. Perhaps because it was not possible to remedy this situation and avoid this pathology, doctors wrote theses on the prevention of death in cases of eclampsia. I was angry because women were not being monitored during pregnancy, that is to say, the medical establishment was not doing what was necessary to avoid hypertension and the risk of death.

I did not want to pursue a career as a doctor, but as a psychoanalyst. To tell the truth, I had only studied medicine to fulfill the wishes of my father, himself a doctor, who saw no other way for his daughter. Like many men of his generation, he wanted me to exercise a respectable profession—such as a doctor, engineer, or lawyer—which was the only conceivable option at the time for a Brazilian woman "from a good family." So, I went that route.

When I was a child and teenager, my father taught me to cultivate my body and compete in sports while I also devoted myself to studying. He died at the age of forty-eight, while I was in my third year of college, but not without teaching me how to care for a terminally ill man—him. More than once, I gave him the necessary injection. In the end, I was the one who prescribed the morphine. So, I had to bear the death of a young father who left me with the moral responsibility for the family: I was the oldest child and also a medical student.

This precocious maturity gave me some audacity. Among other things, I joined the movement opposed to the military dictatorship in 1969, and then left Brazil four years later to begin my training with Lacan, which meant separating from my partner at the time—who, due to his work obligations, was not able to accompany me—and finding myself alone in a city whose culture I did not know and whose language I did not speak.

The fact is that I gave priority to analytical training. I did not imagine that it was going to cost me my marriage. My boyfriend was not one who could wait or say "your date will be mine": he chose sex over love. Without any real attachment to me, he was in no position to accept my freedom. He was a chauvinist without knowing it, and I did not know it either.

Love happens between similar people, and machismo can only be contrary to it, since it does not allow for female desire. Caetano Veloso expresses this in a song: "He is the one who wants/He is the man/I am only the woman." Other lyrics by Chico Buarque clearly state how a woman should behave: "in your presence I keep silent/by day I am a flower/by night I am your horse/his beer is sacred/his will is the most just."

Machismo culture was rampant in Brazil, a country that never ceased to rank high on the scale of rape and femicide. Women and children are the first victims of this culture, but so are men. They unwittingly obey the evil imperative of revenge and become criminals.

Before my trip, I wrote twice to Lacan to tell him that I wanted to come to France. I fixed the date when I received his telegram.

> "Alright, dear Madame, I am making arrangements now to
>   receive you at your convenience.
> Yours truly,
> Jacques Lacan
> P.S. Specify to me as you can the (specific) date of your arrival."

DOCTEUR JACQUES LACAN   à D. a. Elizabeth MILAN
ANCIEN CHEF DE CLINIQUE À LA FACULTÉ
5. RUE DE LILLE. VII⁵
LITTRÉ 30-01   SUR RENDEZ-VOUS

Entendu, chère Madame, je prends mes

dispositions dès maintenant pour vous

reçevoir à votre grê.

                    Croyez-moi votre

P.S - Précisez-moi dès que vous le pourrez

la date(précise)de votre arrivée.

Ce 24.I.73

Figure 1 Telegram from Lacan to author (1973).

When I received the telegram, I did not immediately realize the curious repetition in the postscript. Did it not betray the Doctor's anticipation? It only hastened my trip.

I prepared with the help of my mother who, for various reasons, fantasized about Paris. She—like many of her contemporaries—was so fascinated by the City of Light that she saw the constellation of the Eiffel Tower in Brazil's sky and the Notre-Dame in the São Paulo cathedral, which, "in addition to its two Gothic towers, has a rose window." There is no doubt that this fascination had to do with the influence of French fashion, which I was completely indifferent to at the time. In Brazil, those who considered themselves Leftists did not care about how they dressed. Our concerns were of another nature, and it was only in Paris that I discovered fashion.

During my preparations, despite the sunny presence emanating from the Doctor, I was a little cold in my soul. I anticipated nostalgia for the place where I had always lived and where nothing was foreign to me.

I WANT TO DO AN ANALYSIS

The day after my arrival, I called the Doctor to tell him that I was in Paris. His response stunned me.

"So what?"

How could Lacan react like this? I had crossed the ocean for him! The fact is that I responded *I want to do an analysis*, clearly confessing my desire. With a simple question, he precipitated the expected answer. He immediately set me an appointment for the next day and hung up.

I stayed with the phone in my hand until I realized that the essentials had been said. By hanging up with a snap, he had made me hear my desire. It is obvious that the Doctor had proceeded in this way because he sensed that there would not be a rupture. Thanks to his clinical experience, he had made abruptness a terribly effective analytical spring.

This phone call was the first session of the second stage of the analysis. It conveys that in a surprisingly short time one can make something decisive happen through the precipitation of desire and through a well-timed interruption—in this case, immediately after having scheduled the second session.

The Doctor was not there for parlor conversation, what he called *empty speech*, but for me to enter into analysis as soon as possible. The space of the consulting room was designed so that *full speech*— meaningful speech for the analysand whose subjective history was treated as an epic—would come to the surface. Everyone was entitled to their own epic narrative.

Lacan sometimes made use of empathy to incite the analysand to enter into analysis, but he could also distance himself to oblige you to move forward. His *modus operandi* was undoubtedly paradoxical, yet it was faithful to the logic of the unconscious, which ignores contradiction. The Doctor's word could serve as a carrot as well as a stick. Each analysand found in him the analyst they deserved.

For the next session, I arrived right on time. But I was not admitted right away. How could it be otherwise, since the duration of the session was a function of the discourse of the analysand and not of chronological time? With the Doctor, the wait was justified, and I never met anyone who took offense. If you wanted to do an analysis with Lacan, you had to accept his method. It is even possible to hypothesize that the time spent in the waiting room was a prerequisite, necessary for what would be said in the session.

I was the third person to be called in.

"Come on in."

In the office, on one side there was the couch and, behind it, a huge armchair with mother-of-pearl inlays. On the other side, in front of a window overlooking the courtyard, there were two small velvet armchairs for *face-to-face* meetings, which precede the passage to the couch. The Doctor pointed to one and sat on the other.

As soon as we were seated, I heard the *Tell me*, which would be repeated throughout the years. It was not the subject of thought that was important, but the subject of the unconscious, which could only reveal itself through speech. It was necessary to pass from *I think, therefore I am* to *I say, therefore I am*.

"I can stay in Paris for four months now."
"What?"
"Four months, like I told you."
"Your French poses a problem."

Why had the Doctor waited so long to tell me? After all, he had already met me and made it clear that he wanted me to come back. But in *your French poses a problem*, I sensed a challenge and responded accordingly.

"Give me some time."

My answer did not convince him.

"I could send you to a Portuguese colleague settled here in Paris."

Lacan only made this proposal because he was unaware of the relationship of the Brazilians with the Portuguese, who had become an object of ridicule for having colonized Brazil. It was pure xenophobia, but I did not realize this. The fact is that transference would not have been possible with an analyst from Portugal. The analyst occupies the position of the *subject supposed to know*, and for historical reasons, a Portuguese woman would not have been suitable in my case.

Moreover, the language spoken in Brazil is not really the same as in Portugal. Apart from lexical dimensions, Brazilians linger on the vowels whereas the Portuguese pronunciation is syncopated. In addition, since the Modernist Movement of 1922, the written language of Brazil has been aligned with the spoken language, and people used to make fun of those who telephoned Portugal "to find out how it's written." So, I vehemently refused the Doctor's proposal.

"If not with you, I'm taking the plane back tonight to Brazil."
"Well, then come back tomorrow."

Lacan, whose motto was *above all, avoid the rupture* [*primo non rompere*], took seriously the *I'm taking the plane back tonight*. He understood that the absolute condition of my desire was him, and that I would not do an analysis if this condition was not satisfied. Moreover, he knew that the language of the unconscious is not the native language, that languages interpenetrate each other and that the signifier of desire imposes itself.

Another analyst might have argued that the analysis must necessarily be done in the mother tongue. But Lacan, in the great humanist tradition, was anything but dogmatic, and by privileging desire he created an opening for resonant and unusual experiences. He accepted the analysis and the gift that I had brought from Brazil: a comb made by the indigenous people of the Amazon, which I later found in his office when it became a museum.

At the next session, he wanted to know if I was descended from indigenous people—a curiosity that surprised me. I had never even seen an indigenous person and had little interest in our native culture.

The origin of São Paulo cannot be dissociated from the catechesis of the indigenous people by the Jesuits, nor from the fact that Tupi-Guarani was spoken there until the eighteenth century. My home city did not interest me despite the richness of its history. São Paulo has always been indifferent to its past with its beautiful colonial buildings, which first gave way to neoclassical architecture, and then to skyscrapers, as the city saw itself as the equal of New York. Wealthy Paulistas rarely traveled to other states in the country. São Paulo was Brazil all to itself. We went to Europe to shop and brought back *know-how*—even if, most of the time, this *know-how* had already gone out of fashion abroad.

The Doctor was not aware of all these things, nor could he have been. I satisfied his curiosity about my origins by reminding him that my ancestors were all Lebanese, all immigrants.

"And what else?"
"Here in France, I'm all alone. I don't know anyone. I stumble over
     every word ... people don't understand what I say. If I don't speak
     quite right, the message doesn't get through."
"Hmm ..."

I had just arrived and was already complaining. The Doctor immediately intervened, underlining the dramatic aspect of my words.

"It's been a big jump. You have crossed from one continent to another.
     As if to discover America!"

He gave an epic dimension to what was only a trip to France, transforming it into an exploit and likening it to a Discovery. Indeed, I was going to discover a new Brazil, the popular culture of which had been alien to me until then. Before my analysis, only French culture mattered to me. Like most Paulista intellectuals of my generation, I was not interested in the cultural peculiarities of my native country. For us, it was a question of absorbing everything that was happening in Paris, of sharing a "reheated" European culture.

If I had not gone to France to work with Lacan, who left no subject unexplored, I would have never gone from my office to watch the carnival artists. The famous Brazilian carnival, which announces the beginning of Lent, entails opulent parades, which in the southeastern cities, such as Rio de Janeiro and São Paulo, are led by samba schools. I started attending the parades because Joãosinho Trinta—the director of the Rio parades—made a statement in the mainstream press: "Only intellectuals like poverty, the poor people like luxury." The phrase was a response to critics who claimed that the carnival parades were a luxury that the country could not afford. To find out what Trinta's retort meant, I went to Rio to meet him.[1]

I heard Trinta say excitedly that only those who lived in palaces or large mansions complained about the presence of floats in the Rio

---

1. I devoted three years of research to the samba schools of Rio de Janeiro. My book *Rio, dans les coulisses du carnaval* (L'Aube, 1998) is a poetic evocation of the festival that emphasizes the "anthropophagic" character of Brazilian popular culture.

Sambodrome: the venue for the parades. But the people who lived in hovels without space, along unpaved streets, demanded the grandiose— experiences of another dimension—which could only be found in the parade. Their luxury was not money but jewelry. Even if the jewels were fake, they were the most genuine parts of their lives because of their magical charge. As Trinta put it, "When she is dressed like a grand duchess, a maid is part of nobility; she is the lady she wants to be. Her jewels are the most authentic, they are those of her imagination."

For the carnival artist—as for Baudelaire—the imagination is undoubtedly the queen of faculties. Among all the riches of the world, Baudelaire preferred "the monsters" of his fantasy.

The carnival represents the worship of an illusion, of a fantasy that governed not only the conquest but also the colonization of Brazil: one of finding paradise or of having already reached it. In this fashion, without ever being the same, the carnival functions by rediscovering an ancestral fantasy, inseparable from the attraction of mystery and wonder.

Thanks to the carnival artists, I discovered that the carnival is not only a day of oblivion but also above all a festival through which Brazil remembers its history and never stops reinventing itself. It appropriates the representations of the East and the West by devouring them like the anthropophagous. It does not imitate, but it plays freely with the representations to create others, always new and always surprising. It is a worship of laughter and transience, which spreads joy everywhere in order to exalt life.

The decision to do my analysis with Lacan and no one else meant that I needed to deepen my French and to be able to speak it fluently as soon as possible. So, I started reading, day and night. I started with *In Search of Lost Time*, but without going further than the first volume, and with difficulty. This universe was too strange for me. I do not know how I discovered Céline's *Journey to the End of the Night*, but this book immediately carried me away. Maybe because Bardamu, the text's anti-hero, is also a doctor. Or because of the stylized orality of the language that characterizes the literature of my country ever since its writers have broken with the literary conventions of Portugal.

In order not to be alone at the hotel all the time, I spent long hours reading at a bistro, with an incredible feeling of freedom. In Brazil, it was impossible to sit alone in a bar without being bothered. It was a space reserved for men or couples.

Analysis was the main reason I came to Paris. But as I progressed in the language, Parisian life became an increasingly crucial factor. The streets were safe and the city was open to me. With each step, a discovery pushed me to take an interest in its history. Without realizing it, I was gradually detaching myself from Brazil where the military dictatorship continued to imprison, torture, and kill.

I did not miss my country. Many of my friends had been forced into exile by the military dictatorship. In France, I escaped the burden of my origins.

As a child, I felt perfectly integrated into my Lebanese family, surrounded by my parents, my many uncles, and all my grandparents. As a teenager, I was a victim of the xenophobia of my peers. They called me a *little Turk*—as if it was not because of the Turks that the Lebanese had to emigrate—and excluded me from events reserved for "four-hundred-year-old Brazilians," descendants of the first settlers. For their part, my ancestors had nothing but contempt for the natives. My paternal grandfather, originally from a village in Mount Lebanon, never ceased to contrast their four short centuries with his four thousand years of civilization.

How could I, who loved my grandfather so much, not be critical of those he criticized? My ancestors had conquered a place in the sun in a land of immigrants and had passed important values on to me—notably the taste for knowledge—but they could not recognize themselves in the country that they had bequeathed to me. I struggled with this as well.

I came to mention this indirectly during a session.

"I'm not sure I like my country."
"Really?"
"Yes."
"Tell me ... I'm listening."
"Actually, I don't know why I come here."
"Hmm ..."
"I have the impression that I am obliged to come."
"Yes, that's right!" replied the Doctor, staring at me.
"But who is forcing me?"
"Tell me, my dear."
"If I only I knew ... wanting is not being able."
"That is also true."

With that sentence, the Doctor got up and said, *See you tomorrow.*

The words were ahead of me. It was only afterwards that I understood their meaning, *Nachträglich.*

My maternal grandmother, whose father had become wealthy after emigrating, spent a year in Paris choosing the furniture for her home. As soon as you entered the house, there was Sèvres porcelain and furniture imported from France. My ancestors were all Maronites and could not but idealize France.

After the fall of the Ottoman Empire at the end of the First World War, the League of Nations mandate made Lebanon a French protectorate. Already in the seventeenth century, Maronite Christians and the French had a close relationship. During the reign of Louis XIV, most of the French consuls in Beirut were Maronites. This gave them a higher social status and they saw France as a friendly country as well as a protector. This is also why I was in Paris, to fulfill the desire of my ancestors. Hence the word *obliged*, which the Doctor had emphasized.

This session illustrates the reason for the substitution of *I say, therefore I am* for *I think, therefore I am.* If Lacan had asked me why I was no longer sure of anything, he would have led me to think. But he reacted by saying *Really?* and then *Tell me, I am listening,* precipitating the word. He knew that the unconscious manifests itself through free association and not through the exercise of thought. With the word *obliged*, I accessed family history and discovered a profound motivation for my journey.

Lacan did not interpret my speech by attributing this or that meaning to it. When he perceived that the unconscious had expressed itself, he sent me back to the solitude of the street so that I could interpret myself. By valorizing free association, this session highlighted both the eminently Freudian character of the Doctor's practice and the validity of the substitution of patient for analysand. If the patient does not reflect on what she has said, the analysis cannot take place. Everyone gets the analyst they deserve …

The analysis was not always easy, and I decided to travel, to take a "vacation from the unconscious." But how to tell the Doctor? I was in France for four months to work with him and I had no serious reason to avoid it. I thought the Doctor was going to refuse me, as my father would have. This did not happen.

"Good, my dear, and when will I see you again?"

I could not believe my ears and, truth be told, I was rather indignant. Was it possible that he did not even ask me why I was away? Was he so indifferent?

I stayed for a long time without saying anything.

"I'll be back in fifteen days."

"Fifteen days?"

With that, the Doctor got up, and I settled the session as usual, putting two hundred francs on his desk, and left. I must say that I did not understand anything and that it is only now, while writing these lines, that I measure the relevance of his answer. By simply asking when he would see me again, he acknowledged my desire and expressed his desire to continue the work.

Lacan was not there to respond to a demand for unconditional love, but for the analysand to stop being contrary to herself, to assume her desire, and to become the subject of her own history.

I traveled without leaving Paris, discovering the monuments indicated by my travel guide and participating in the guided tours offered by *Pariscope*. What impressed me the most was the relationship of Parisians to their past, the emphasis on everything the city has to offer, even the sewer system where Jean Valjean, the protagonist of *Les Misérables*, had taken refuge.

On the one hand, Paris left me speechless. On the other hand, it forced me to realize the contempt that Brazil has for memory. From one day to the next, the buildings that told its story were, and still are, ruthlessly demolished to make way for others in the name of money and efficiency. Or they catch fire through neglect, as happened in 2018 when the National Museum of Rio, the former residence of the emperors of Brazil, whose collections were gathered over two centuries, almost completely disappeared. Among these collections was Luzia, the oldest human fossil found in South America, dating from some thirteen thousand years ago.

When the group tour was over, I wandered around the city admiring the facades of the buildings and the carved wooden gates with motifs that I was trying to decipher—which is why I always carried a small dictionary of mythology with me. When I was not walking in the streets, I went to the quays to enjoy the landscape, the barges which some Parisians had made their residence, the plane trees, and the weeping willows. By its color of cane juice, the Seine reminded me of my childhood in Brazil.

Every time I passed by Place du Châtelet, I admired the gilded statue of Victory, with her exuberant breasts and hips, her open arms, a laurel wreath in each hand. I saw in her an exaltation of the female figure and a symbol of the City of Light—perhaps because of the gilding ...

It was another Victory that had awakened in me, at eighteen, the fantasy of visiting Paris, the Victory of Samothrace, a powerful figurehead that stands at the top of a staircase in the Louvre. I took advantage of my "vacation from the unconscious" to go once again to the museum to contemplate that winged woman, in whom I saw a brilliant representation of female freedom.

While visiting Paris, I realized how much the city still had to offer me. Yet before this parenthesis in the analysis ended, I had already returned to the Doctor's office. It was the day after a dream that had reoccurred, and I needed to tell him about it.

"Tell me."

"I dreamed of you in my country."

"Interesting."

"A real feast, a banquet ... you and I were sitting atop a mango tree."

"A what?"

"A mango tree ... but we were eating sapodilla, a fruit that does not exist here ... There were three of us, you, me and a black angel with a crown of ipê flowers, a tree from there."

"Hmm ..."

"You were spelling the words in Portuguese."

"So, I went from French to Portuguese!"

"And what's more, you went to heaven with the angel."

"On the way to a better world ..."

The Doctor got up with his *See you tomorrow*, and I wondered why he had not encouraged me to make associations that would have allowed me to interpret the dream. On the way home, I remembered a passage from *The Interpretation of Dreams* in which Freud recalls a dream from Anna, his daughter, then one and a half years old. The little girl had made herself sick by eating too many strawberries and could not eat all day. The next night, in her sleep, she had recited an entire menu: "Strawberries, wild strawberries, omelet, pudding." For Freud, this was proof that a dream is a fulfillment of a desire.

Desire is expressed directly in childhood dreams and the interpretation does not require the dreamer's associations. My dream of feasting with the Doctor was like that of children. It expressed my desire to continue the analysis with him in Brazil and in Portuguese. This was to be expected, and Lacan had foreseen it. Nevertheless, this was out of the realm of possibility. The work was underway and there was no going back. Whether I liked it or not, French would be the language of my analysis, since I could not conceive of any other analyst besides the Doctor.

Of the four months I was to spend in France, only one remained. In addition to the analysis, I read the Doctor's seminars and the authors to whom he was making references. That year, in his first lecture, Lacan said that the title of the seminar could just as well be *Les non-dupes errent* [*The Non-Dupes Err*] as *Les noms du père* [*The Names of the Father*]. So, he began with a play on words, highlighting the ambiguity of language and Freud's work on the relationship between wordplay and the unconscious.

In his approach, Lacan always came back to Freud and free association, which encourages the analysand to say freely whatever comes to mind, even if it means getting lost. This is the condition for the unconscious to manifest itself. Moreover, I retained from this seminar a sentence that helped me to pursue my own approach: "We must not understand too quickly."

Unlike other forms of knowledge which exclude the subject in the name of objectivity, it is precisely on the subject that the knowledge of the unconscious rests. But this knowledge needs to be deciphered. Like the sphinx, the unconscious presents us with riddles and demands patience. This is no doubt why Lacan recommended crossword puzzles to analysts.

I do not remember all the sessions during these four months, but I have never forgotten the last one, thanks to the very unexpected intervention of the Doctor.

Willy-nilly, I had packed my bags. I had to resume my clinic in Brazil, where my companion was supposed to be waiting for me. Despite the cold, I went for a stroll before the session: the sunny day was an invitation to walk. At the Châtelet, I stopped once more at the foot of the Victory statue before going through the Tuileries Garden. I wanted to see the women of Maillol again, his erotic sculptures, and the one whose gesture seems to repel those who approach. I would also miss them in Brazil, where the exhibition of the female body serves enjoyment and not contemplation. Could the worship of femininity exist in a country that has never known courtly love?

I walked from the garden to the Doctor's office, where the waiting room, for once, was empty. He received me quickly.

"Come on in, my dear."

"This is the last session …"

"Hmm …"

"If I have to take stock of what has happened, I can't say what I have
    done here or why I am leaving … What good will it do me to have
    worked with such a famed [*renommé*] analyst?"

"Tell me …"

"If I knew, I would tell you."

Silence.

"I only know one thing, it's my dream from yesterday."

"Yes … I am listening."

"I dreamed that I asked you something."

"What was it?"

"I was asking you to read the name of a street in Brazil."

"Interesting … fame, name [*renom, nom*] … Perhaps you will make a
    name from my fame [*un nom de mon renom*] …"

The Doctor made an association concluded by a play on words. He always resorted to it in the session as in the seminar.

The fact is that I left satisfied. Lacan knew how important the question of the name was for me, a descendant of immigrants. In addition to losing their land of origin, those who emigrate start their lives again elsewhere with a name that means nothing. They are nothing more than an outsider.

The Doctor bet on my desire to become a psychoanalyst recognized for her work and, moreover, for her work *with him*. That is to say, he bet on his own desire. For Lacan, as for Freud, the transmission of psychoanalysis was fundamental. He wanted to have disciples, so why not in Brazil?

I WANT TO BE A MOTHER

Contrary to what I had imagined, the return to Brazil was a disaster. My companion had met another woman and had no intention of leaving her. In my desperation, I started drinking and was seized by an obsession: I had to get revenge. Without realizing, I was reacting like the past Brazilian women whose husbands cheated on them with one of their slaves. They abandoned themselves to cruelty beyond measure, breaking the servant's teeth with their heels, slashing her breasts, or burning her ears.

This violence was not like me; it indicated a deep imbalance. Faced with this situation, my mother convinced me to return to France and resume work with Lacan. She sensed that my condition also had to do with the interruption of the analysis.

Bending to her will, I left without a clear plan. The plane stopped in Liberia, a country I knew nothing about, but where I wanted to stay. I was completely disoriented. I wanted to delay Paris and even more so the Doctor. I had not even told him that I was coming back. What was I going to tell him now? That I was obsessed with revenge? That I was capable of committing a crime? I did not want to discredit myself, but these thoughts made me feel so powerful that I did not want to give them up.

In Paris, I first lived in the subway. Consumed by a jealousy that fed on itself, I was going from one station to another, constantly moving to be nowhere, among strangers to be with no one. Sometimes I remembered the Doctor's pun—*Perhaps you will make a name from my fame.* Now it paralyzed me. All I had done in Brazil was to separate from my companion and battle with a rival; I had done nothing for the noble cause of psychoanalysis.

It took me a while to decide and only a double whiskey allowed me to go to rue de Lille without telling anyone. Gloria was getting to know me; she opened the door and showed me to the waiting room. I imagine the Doctor was surprised to see me, but he did not let it show. He just waved me in. He was not one of those who only received by appointment and resisted analysis. He encouraged me to keep coming.

"Speak."
"But say what?"
"Whatever you want."

He understood that I was afraid, so he continued.

"Nothing you say will leave here."
"I only went to Brazil to come back."
"What do you mean?"
"Paris is all I have left."

Without asking me why, the Doctor came up with an unexpected answer.

"I cannot make any guarantees."
"I didn't ask you."
"You assume the entire risk."
"Yes, I know."
"Then, see you tomorrow."

The Doctor challenged me. This is what I needed to abandon the position of being humiliated and offended, to regain my self-esteem. Lacan knew how to evaluate the degree of transference—maximum in my case—and to act accordingly. This session shows to what extent the treatment relies on the sensitivity of the analyst and why Lacan said that psychoanalysis is an art. In these two fields, intuition, the capacity to comprehend without reasoning, *to get it* (*de piger*), is fundamental.

Lacan had gotten me back into the process of analysis in a few words. This third phase from 1974 to 1976 would be the longest and the most decisive. During this period, I would confront the double question of origins and motherhood, and I would leave the comfort of the mother tongue to translate the master.

My father always challenged me to go above and beyond. This is probably why *You assume the entire risk* of the Doctor worked. It also highlights two of Lacan's recourses as an analyst. By going against expectations, in a moment of crisis, he could say to the analysand *Don't count on me*, encouraging her to count on herself. He used the challenge as a remedy for depression. The other recourse was paradox. On the one hand, *I*

cannot make any guarantees, but on the other, *See you tomorrow*. Like
the unconscious, Lacan ignored contradiction.

So, I rented an apartment in Paris to continue the analysis. Of course,
it was in the Latin Quarter where I walked to rue de Lille.

It was because of another session during this third stage that I
submitted a project to teach in the Department of Psychoanalysis at
the University of Vincennes, directed by Lacan. The session in question
had to do with a pendant I was wearing at the time: a glass eye framed
with silver lids, a jewel made by an Eastern European whose art I
admired for the original combination of metals and materials from
Brazil.

That day, the Doctor did not sit in the large armchair as usual. He
remained standing in front of me, staring at me with a slight sway of
his body.

"Tell me."
"With you there, so close, I can't say anything."

He did not sit down, though, and continued to look at me before
speaking.

"What do you wear around your neck?"
"An eye."
"A fetish ..."
"Maybe, but I never thought of it that way. It's a piece of jewelry I
    like."
"What else?"
"I'm going to take the exam to teach in the Department of
    Psychoanalysis."
"On what subject?"
"I don't know yet, but I'll be submitting a proposal soon."
"Very well, go ahead ... See you tomorrow, my dear."

I walked out wondering about the Doctor's bizarre remark. What
did the glass eye have to do with a fetish? I remembered the Eye of
Horus that I had seen in the Egyptian Art Department of the Louvre. It
symbolized power and warded off the *evil eye*. The Eye of Horus made
me think of the fetishes brought to Brazil by African slaves who never
renounced their beliefs and rituals—hence the religious syncretism of
Brazil.

Like other children of my social background, I had been educated by my parents, but raised by a woman of African descent—the eternal domestic worker—who told me stories about magic. Her name was Maria. I did not leave the house without my eye necklace. How could I not conclude, after the session, that it was indeed a fetish and that I believed in its protective power? I believed in it without being aware of it, my scientific training being incompatible with magic.

Whether I liked it or not, African culture was also mine. On the one hand, I had grown up listening to the stories of *Arabian Nights*, told by my Lebanese grandfather. On the other hand, I had heard Maria tell me her stories of spells, saying that the fetish protected against the *evil eye* and made the body *invulnerable*. I might only have Lebanese ancestry, but culturally I was a *mestiza*.

Because he stared at my pendant, the Doctor led me to define the theme of the project I was going to present to the Department of Psychoanalysis at the University of Vincennes: it would be fetishism. I wanted to go further into the meaning of fetishism in psychoanalytic theory and in Brazilian religious syncretism, to which I had been introduced by a friend, who was a dramatist. She had told me more than once about the effects of black magic to ward off a rival. We went together to a center in Rio where the mother of a saint, Vovo Conga de Angola, had the power to undo all black magic work. We stayed there for hours, waiting for the mysterious grandmother. Her presence was continuously announced and then postponed. In a space teeming with roosters and stray dogs, we could only see the light of candles. Everything was permeated with the smell of smoke.

It was a first experience with magic, and it taught me how power can be established through taking advantage of expectation and mystery to reinforce belief.[1] From that moment, I made countless trips across the country as an apprentice-tourist in order to better know the Afro-Brazilian worshippers. I was even able to attend the secret worship of the ancestors of Bahia, whose ritual renders some ancestral spirits visible. They are called Egun, Baba Egun, or Baba. This was an important reference at the end of my analysis.[2]

1. On this topic, I have written *Diabolavida* (*Ornicar*, revue du Champ freudien, #6, March 1975).
2. The worship of the ancestors, *Ilé Agbóula*, takes place on the island of Itaparica in Bahia.

Thanks to all these travels, I was able to overcome the xenophobia of my ancestors, perhaps related to the fact that when they arrived in Brazil, they had to suffer it themselves. Decades later, so as not to be called a *little Turk*, I began to obscure my origins. I would say, for example, that my father's name was Ricardo instead of Rachid, a fact that later surfaced in the analysis.

Already at the time, because of immigration, having an Arabic name was not easy. The terrorist threat has only made the situation worse. Much later, when my son was born, I refused to give him a name that would reveal his Arab origins, despite my husband's insistence.

Paris is made for the eyes. It is an invitation to see and to be seen. There are mirrors everywhere—on the facades of buildings, in restaurants, in bars ... There is no way to neglect your appearance. The apartment I rented was in an eighteenth-century building on rue de la Harpe, and there was a mirror in every room. I knew how to enjoy them. I studied my outfits: the old ones, the new ones, and the future ones. In the midst of Parisian women, I wanted to become elegant. Before, I could not have imagined it.

The fashion demanded a model's figure, but because of a large posterior, my body defied it. I had to negotiate with my body and with fashion until I could satisfy the woman I was discovering. The mirror helped me not to fool myself; it helped me not to wear clothes that did not suit me. I needed the image to find my style. This I knew. Yet it was in a session that I discovered why the mirror fascinated me.

> "I have moved into my new house ... It's a lady's apartment; I call her Madame, but she prefers to be called Mademoiselle. A sixty-year-old lady who says she's in love ... The apartment is bright and there are mirrors everywhere ... actually, I wish there were more."
> "Really?"

After a silence, I continued to speak, evoking Versailles, which I had visited the week before.

> "The Hall of Mirrors ... The windows, the view of the gardens ... I'll go back as soon as I can."
> "Tell me more ... I'm listening."
> "Louis XIV dreamed in my place."
> "How?"

The tone of his voice denoted perplexity. I repeated what I had said.

"Louis XIV, the Sun King."

At this point, the Doctor cut the session to have me listen to myself. What I had said was peculiar, and he highlighted this peculiarity in order to give importance to my speech. How could the Sun King have dreamed instead of a Brazilian woman? For Lacan, peculiarity was a sign that the unconscious was manifesting itself, a sign that he always took into account in his practice.

Louis XIV had dreamed for me, because my maternal grandmother and my mother dreamed aloud of royalty. The ancestors' dream was mine and I too liked to imagine being a queen or a princess. So, I could only be in my place at Versailles in the Hall of Mirrors. This fascination comes straight from that of the Lebanese for the reign of Louis XIV and of the Brazilians for the monarchy. It is no coincidence that our carnival abounds with kings, queens, princesses, and knights. "To be a queen for a day, that's what we poor people want," said one character from La Mangueira, a large samba school in Rio. "To shine in gold, in lamé, in silver, in precious stones …" This is the desire of those who come down from the favela—the shantytown on the outskirts of the city—to take possession of the city. With the luxury of the imagination, they make Rio the theater of a spectacle as grandiose as it is unusual, worthy of the Sun King's wildest dreams.

This question of the mirror was secondary. What interested me was psychoanalytic theory and the elaboration of my teaching project on fetishism, based on Freud's 1905 text, *Three Essays on the Theory of Sexuality*. But writing in French complicated my life. If I spoke it now without any problem, writing it was a completely different matter. It irritated me deeply, and I went to the session reluctantly. I had no desire to talk.

With another analyst, I could have remained silent during the whole session—as if he and I were only there to show up. With Lacan, this was impossible. He carried the desire to listen and did not allow me to remain silent, or rather to remain silent so as not to complain.

"Tell me."
"If I could …"

The Doctor thought I was afraid of something and told me again that he was not there to censor me.

"It's not because I'm afraid to speak. But because the word that comes
    to me does not exist in your language."
"What do you mean?"
"It simply does not exist."
"What is this word?"
" ... *Saudade.*"

He immediately interrupted the session.

With the word *saudade* and my native language at heart, the Doctor
let me go. After having spoken Portuguese without being aware of
my relationship with the language—like most Brazilians—I had just
realized that it was in this language, and in this language only, that I was
walking on solid ground. How many sessions did it take me to reach
this new awareness!

My language was Brazilian-Portuguese and I wanted to live in
it. But I did not want to go back to São Paulo. A city that devoured
itself and consumed all memories, razing the colonial villas to build
skyscrapers ... a city without limits that was indifferent to its streets and
squares, crossed by a nauseating river, an open, dark sewer.

In the days following the *saudade* session, I dreamed more than once
of Maria. In the first dream, she offered a mirror to a red figurine whose
breasts and sex were prominent. It could only be the Pomba Gira, a
spiritual figure of the Umbanda who circulates between the world of
African divinities and that of the living. Arriving in Brazil with the
slaves of Bantu origin, she has become a powerful erotic symbol that
manifests through a medium: a person through which the Pomba Gira
is incarnated.[3]

In the second dream, Pomba Gira appeared with a wide skirt, lace
blouse, and many necklaces. Maria offered her a bottle of *pinga* and
told her: "Drink, I want to see." What she wanted was for Pomba Gira
to start dancing. Through her desire for eroticism, it was my own that
was expressed.

Following these two dreams, I had a third where Maria was reading
my future in cowrie shells, a dream I wanted to talk about during the
session. But since the Doctor knew nothing of the Umbanda, the Pomba
Gira, or the cowries, mentioning it made little sense.

---

3. The medium is a figure of the Umbanda but also of Spiritism which has
spread in the United States.

Instead of sitting down as I always did, immediately when I entered the office that day, I lay down on the couch. Lacan did not flinch. Without saying anything, he settled behind me in the large armchair.

"So, what is it, my dear?"
"I can't talk about what I want to tell you."
"Hmm …"
"Does the Pomba Gira mean anything to you?"

He obviously did not answer this provocative question. He was not there to get into a power struggle with me or any other analysand.

"Interesting …"
"You don't answer, you just say *interesting*. I don't understand anything anymore. I'm disoriented. Really, I wonder what I'm doing here."
"Hmm …"
"I miss Maria … my language … my country. In fact, I …"
"Yes, tell me."
"In fact, I'm only here because of you."

I broke down in tears. Lacan stood up, all at once.

"There is no reason to despair. You have masterfully taken possession of this couch! Now, it is yours."

A few words of comfort, said in a theatrical manner, and I was turned around. Having me understand at once that I was there for my analytic training and that I had just taken an important step, Lacan took me from desolation to satisfaction. And a little later, I was going to find a solution to continue working with him without giving up my mother tongue.

That day, I left the office repeating the Doctor's phrases: *You have masterfully taken possession of this couch! Now, it is yours.* What did it mean to go from face to face to the couch? I would no longer see the Doctor; I would always lay there with my eyes on the ceiling, and my words would be my only existence. As for him, he would only be present to listen to what I said. It would be a relationship based exclusively on speech and listening. Or rather, on speech that Lacan treated as a text and on the listening of someone who was reading what was said. Hence, Lacan's substitution of the word *punctuation* for *interpretation*.

I was a little distressed about this new prospect. When I left the office, I went for a walk in the city. I turned right into the rue de Lille, then left into the rue des Saints-Pères, and then crossed toward the Seine, which each time revitalized me. I stopped for a while on the Pont-Neuf to look at the stone masks that Henri IV had sculpted to ridicule his ministers who doubted the solidity of the bridge.

The move to the couch was a turning point in the analysis and quickly bore fruit. On very hot summer days, there were rats in the streets of Paris. But it was not just any rat that I saw on the ground floor of the building where I lived; it was an enormous, truly frightening one. I asked the caretaker to come and see.

"A big rat? Where?"
"Here, on the ground floor ..."
"I don't see anything."
"There ... it is hiding under the stairs."

The caretaker looked, then turned toward me, annoyed.

"There's nothing there at all, Miss. The building has been sanitized, and besides, I'm very busy."

With that he left and I went to my session. How could I be so sure that I had seen a rat that the caretaker denied existed? Was it a hallucination? Had I perceived something that did not exist? I had to conclude that this was the case. If I told the doctor, he would take me for a psychotic ...

Halfway there, I considered not going ... not running the risk of being banished from the group of future analysts. As if an analyst could not have any symptoms, as if the symptom could not be treated. My fear was that of those who still did not believe enough in the "talking cure." That is why I was a candidate and not an analyst.

The waiting room was full, but probably because of the expression on my face, the Doctor saw me right away.

"Come on in."

As soon as I lay down, I told him what had happened. But I hid behind my psychiatric training, trying to show that I knew the cause.

"I had a hallucination."
"What?"
"Yes, a visual hallucination."

The Doctor did not give importance to the symptom. He was interested in the object of the hallucination.

"And what did you see?"
"A rat ... an enormous rat."
"What?"
"A rat, *um rato*."

As I repeated the word, the first syllable took on sudden importance and I made an unexpected association.

"*Ra* is the first syllable of the name ..."
"Tell me ..."
"The name of my father, the name that I would not speak."
"Why?"
"So as not to be called a Turk."

At this point, he interrupted the session. It was the name of the father, the object of a permanent denial, which had appeared in the hallucination. It had emerged in reality, and thanks to the cut, which obliged me to listen to myself, it was now impossible for me to deny my origins. The way to overcome auto-xenophobia had been opened.

The episode of the hallucinatory rat once again highlights the reason for the variable-length session. The duration depended on the interruption made by Lacan at the moment he deemed appropriate. It was Kairos that determined it. Moreover, this session allows us to understand why in the *Écrits* he distinguishes logical time from chronological time. Was it not logical to interrupt my speech when the question of origins arose? *Ra* led me to Rachid, the first name of my great-grandfather, my grandfather, and my father. This repetition is linked to the worship of Harun al-Rashid, the caliph who made Baghdad a flourishing cultural center and who is a reference for the entire Eastern World, figuring in several tales of the *Arabian Nights*.

If they had not emigrated, my ancestors could have died because of the war and the rest of us would never have had the right to venerate the saint of our choice. Religious intolerance—although it has not been a constant—is inherent in the history of Lebanon. Born and raised in a country, Brazil, where religions and people have always mixed, I did not know about religious intolerance and did not understand the importance of the diaspora.

My people wanted to forget the past: forgetting was for them the condition for the integration of their descendants. In order to better understand the circumstances of their journey, I interviewed members of my family who agreed to speak. They denied having experienced the tragedy of immigration—their narcissistic wound—and I refused to be who I was: the daughter of immigrants. Hence the dream that followed the session on the hallucinatory rat.

I find myself in an unknown house. The doorbell rings. I look out the window and see a glass carriage. Two black bulls throw themselves against the horses. One of them falls, wounded, and the carriage shatters. I rush into the street. Next to the wounded horse, I find my sister, dead.

I wake up scared, unable to breathe. What could this dream mean? I want my sister to be alive. I know that associations are necessary to access the signified. I cannot make any. I remember Freud. He woke up in the middle of the night, wrote down his dream and his associations to interpret them later. I write down the dream. I will recount it during the next session.

It was impossible for me to sleep and I went out into the city, although it was still dark. I wanted to see the dawn. In Paris, at that time, a woman was not at any risk. I went from rue de la Harpe to the Parvis Notre-Dame and from there to the quays. I needed to soothe myself by contemplating the changing waters of the Seine.

The day of the session arrived and I told my dream.

"What else?"
"What else? My sister and I are physically very similar. I have always
    seen myself in her. In the dream, she is in my place."
"Hmm ..."
"It seems to me that the dream is related to my death ... Why bulls,
    I do not know. The bull, in Greece, was a sacred animal ... It
    symbolized strength. In my language, there is even the expression
    strong like a bull. The glass carriage, on the other hand, is fragile ...
    it shattered."

After a silence, the Doctor called me back.

"Tell me."
"The glass carriage is reminiscent of Cinderella ... She was the one
   who was targeted, a *white*, *blond*, *civilized* woman ... The woman
   I wanted to be."
"How?"
"I always had the fantasy of being blonde ... I never wanted my olive
   skin. The one who died in the dream is Cinderella."
"I'm listening."
"Yes, that's it. The Cinderella that I wanted to be is dead. Now you're
   going to tell me *See you tomorrow*. But I can only come back next
   week."

I gave the date, I paid for the session, and I left. I examined the back
of my hand, the color of those who came from the Mediterranean. I then
remembered an aunt who tried to lighten her skin with egg whites. She
lived in a small village, far from the capital, but thanks to the cinema,
she knew about the existence of blonde Hollywood divas.

To accept the olive color of my skin was not yet to love it. But it had
never occurred to me to lighten my skin like this aunt who lived in
expectation of marriage, tirelessly getting ready for her future husband.
This was like the other women in the family with whom I could never
identify both because of their life plan and their relationship with the
body. They were all bordering on obesity, and I had been raised to be an
athlete. As a teenager, I had participated in swimming competitions and
I worshipped Esther Williams, whose films I loved.

Although I never wanted to be an actress, I was fascinated by the
feminine figure of the Hollywood stars. I do not know how many times
I went to see *Camille* for Greta Garbo, or *Gone with the Wind* to dream
of Vivien Leigh, to hear her say, "Tomorrow is another day ..."

This is what I talked about during the session, perhaps to the Doctor's
surprise.

"The only role I would have liked to play in the cinema is that of
   Greta Garbo ..."
"Which one?"
"*Camille*, I wanted to wear her long dresses ... of white or black tulle."
"What else?"

"I wanted to be on a pedestal, like her. The courtesan does not desire,
     but she is desired."
"It's true."
"*Camille* or Scarlett O'Hara, courted by all, adored by Rhett
     Butler ..."

After a prolonged silence, I said that I did not understand myself,
and the Doctor told me that the session was over. For him, the most
important thing was not to understand, but to speak and then find
the meaning. He firmly believed in the effects of speech and in the
analysand's interpretation. Regarding this, he says in the opening
statement of *Freud's Papers on Technique*, "It behooves the students to
find out for themselves the answer to their own questions. The master
does not teach *ex cathedra* a ready-made science; he supplies an answer
when the students are on the verge of finding it."[4]

In refusing to attribute this or that meaning to the analysand's
speech, Lacan established a watershed. When assigning meaning, the
analyst can provoke resistance and transform analysis into a power
struggle. That is why Lacan says that, in addition to *the resistance of the
analysand*, there is also *the resistance of the analyst*, which is expressed
when the latter hinders the analytic process.

The session mentioned above shows to what extent the knowledge
of the analyst, who accepts ignorance, differs from that of the professor,
who presents himself as the one who knows. In his texts, Freud tirelessly
exposes and corrects his own ideas. His thinking is always subject to
revision; it is that of an eternal seeker. Hence the idea that the analyst
is characterized by a learned ignorance (*ignorantia docta*) and the
insistence on returning to Freud, so that psychoanalytic theory never
loses the force of its origins.

I did not understand the session where I referred to *Gone with the Wind*
until I realized my narcissism, the same narcissism that characterized
Scarlett O'Hara and ultimately made her relationship with Rhett Butler
impossible.

4. Jacques Lacan, *The Seminar of Jacques Lacan, Book I (1953–1954): Freud's
Papers on Technique*, trans. John Forrester (New York: W. W. Norton, 1991),
1 (November 18, 1953).

The difficulty interpreting what happened during this session led me to imagine the Doctor's death. The waiting room was full and suddenly I envisioned that the people present were attending a wake. Despite being dead, the Doctor appeared to bid us farewell (*dire adieu*) and console us.

When my turn came and Lacan appeared in the doorway, I was very uncomfortable. He paused before telling me to *come on in*. I was so much in my fantasy that I wondered if it was the living one or the ghost. It took me a second *come on in* to get up, follow him into his office, and lie down on the couch.

I spoke right away, as if the Doctor could read my mind.

"I don't know what I'm doing with the dead ..."
"Which dead?"
" ... You."
"Hmm ..."
"I'm feeling more and more lost. In the waiting room, I imagined that
    we were all here for your wake. But I don't want you dead. What
    good would it do me?"
"Tell me."
"All I have to say is that today I don't want to talk. I want to leave. I'm
    afraid of the fantasia ... no, no it's not that."
"What is it then?"
"I wanted to say *afraid of the phantom* [*fantôme*] ... I made a mistake
    ... it was a slip of the tongue. I said the word in Portuguese."

The drama of the two languages was recurrent. After the session, I found a solution. I offered to translate one of the Doctor's seminars, *Freud's Papers on Technique*, and, with his approval, I embarked on the adventure.

The seminar was based on Lacan's speech. In other words, the translation had to refer to the oral language. So, it was necessary to imagine how he would have spoken to Brazilians and to write from there. This meant not always respecting grammar. This was the condition for the master's teaching to be accessible in my country.

At the very beginning of the analysis, Lacan had told me: *You have crossed from one continent to another. As if to discover America!* This is precisely what happened thanks to translation. I discovered America through the Portuguese language in which I was going to translate the master before writing my own books.

The first seminar translated and published in Brazil was *Freud's Papers on Technique*. It was an entirely new experience and it was not easy to find the right tone. In order to achieve this, I wrote, read, rewrote, and reread countless times. I proceeded as Lacan recommended, quoting Boileau: "Bring your work back to the workshop twenty times. Polish it continuously, and polish it again."

If the question of tone was problematic, the translation of concepts was no less so. There is the *ça*, for example, which corresponds to the German *es*. The English edition of Freud's complete works, the *Standard Edition*, opted for Latin, with the *id* instead of the *it*. This was a solution in opposition to Freud who drew on his language to designate psychological parts of the mind (*ich* and *es*). Anticipating the astonishment of his readers at the choice of simple German pronouns "instead of pompous Greek names," Freud insisted on the importance of adopting the words of spoken language for his theory. He wished to make scientific use of colloquial language, so that his teachings could be understood by patients "often intelligent, but not always literate."

With Freud's considerations in mind, I went to the session.

"There is nothing more difficult than translating you."
"Hmm ..."
"I don't know how to render the *ça*, which is a translation of the German *es*. In the Portuguese version, the *es* has been translated as *id*, as in the *Standard Edition*. I see no reason to adopt the English solution. That's not what you did in French."
"Yes, exactly."
"Freud shows that the theory must use the words of the language in which it is elaborated. You adopted a pronoun in your language ... it's a return to Freud."
"That's right."

I left the session with the word *isso* in mind, which I would later use to translate the *ça*.

For a long time, the theme of the relationship between languages kept recurring in the analysis, and I felt like I was trapped in it. In everyday life, I would switch from Portuguese to French, but in translation it was the other way around. Both situations were uncomfortable. If I was able to bear it, it was because I loved Paris, its pervasive beauty, and the freedom I had in the city. Apart from a few of Lacan's analyst colleagues and members of the Freudian School of Paris, I knew almost nobody.

I had plenty of time to study, write, and wander without being bothered. In the 1970s, the streets were safe. With the exception of vagabonds, who chose to live on the streets, there were not many homeless people or immigrants without housing. In the Paris of that time, we could imagine Hemingway's *A Moveable Feast* and Henry Miller's *Quiet Days in Clichy*.

One day, after several futile attempts to translate the *ça*, a solution appeared to me. I ran to tell the doctor about it.

> "The translation of the *ça* into Portuguese ... I must take into account the German as well as the French. The *es* is a neutral pronoun ... It belongs to the psychic domain foreign to the ego ..."
> "Yes."
> "It designates what is not personal ... it is an impersonal pronoun."
> "Hmm ..."
> "The *ça* is a substitute for an impersonal pronoun, but also a demonstrative. In French you say *ça ne se fait pas*, which in Portuguese would be *isso não se faz*. Why not translate *ça* as *isso*? The *isso* is demonstrative and functions as an impersonal pronoun."

Lacan stood up and repeated forcefully *that's it, that's it*. His repetition and emphasis proved that my argument had convinced him. As I left the office, I was radiant. If I had not been delivered from myself, I had finally been delivered from the translation of the *ça*, the obligatory point of passage of my analysis. For Lacan, formation presupposed that the analysand was committed to disseminating analytic theory. My translation work validated my commitment.

As if living between two languages was not enough, a dream introduced a third. Maria rocked me as she swayed her body. My mother appeared repeating *iahabibe—my darling*—in Arabic. She approached Maria, and told her *it is time*. She then began to rock me in turn, singing in Arabic. Like all my second-generation ancestors, my mother spoke both Arabic and Portuguese. It was with this recollection that I went to the session.

"My grandparents and parents spoke Arabic, but never taught it
to me."
"Curious."
"They used the language to say what children should not know ... to
hide certain things. But my mother used to rock me in Arabic ...
Except I can't sing like her ..."
"And so?"
"So, nothing."

After a while, the Doctor resorted to his eternal *Tell me*.

"I cannot have a child because I don't know my mother's lullaby."
"Well, for your child, you will invent another one."

His answer set me on a path that I had not foreseen because of an
unconscious fantasy. At the time, I imagined that if I had a child, I
would have to behave exactly like my mother. Lacan let me know what
I would discover only after I had my son: there is no such thing as a
model mother and there cannot be. Each child is unique, it is up to the
mother to invent her relationship with him.

After entering the scene of Arabic, I went to Cairo—a tourist trip—
where I had a dream. My paternal grandfather was wearing a fez
and baggy pants. We were flying over a cemetery on a carpet in slow
motion. He was pointing to the graves and naming the offerings that
the Egyptians made to the dead: statuettes, vases, musical instruments,
food dishes ... The dream made an impression on me and I wanted to
talk about it during the session.

The cemetery was never ending ... A bit like the City of the Dead that
I visited in Cairo. My grandfather emigrated from Lebanon to Brazil,
which would explain his strange outfit. He was a simple man who
spent his life reading. He liked to show us the books he received from
Alexandria and tell us stories. He used to mix Arabic phrases into
them, and his grandchildren were all fascinated. He was a wonderful
storyteller ... One day, he suddenly had a vestibular syndrome and
fainted. My uncles had to carry him to his room ... That scene was
the beginning of his end. I never forgot it.
"What else?"
"My grandfather wanted to teach me Arabic. I learned the numbers
and the alphabet, but that was all. He died of a heart attack. He
had moved to Brazil, but lived in nostalgia for his homeland."

"Hmm ..."
"He passed on this longing for his home country to me."

On that day, I was the one who stood up first, verging on tears. I put the money on the desk and was about to leave when I heard, "Come back tomorrow, dear. I'll be here waiting for you."
Wherever I am, this nostalgia inherited from my grandfather always accompanies me.

When I started translating, I was looking for an impossible identity between French and Portuguese. This was because I had never translated before and also related to my transference towards Lacan. A parallel was established between translation and analysis. The two progressed together towards the end, which only happens when the transference is worked through or the analyst ceases to be the *subject supposed to know*. In my case, this implied that I make the French text my own in Portuguese. This would not be the conquest of America, but that of a new homeland, the homeland of writing, where I felt I was on firm ground.
The Doctor was well aware of this. He let me indulge in the throes of the incessant passage from one language to another without ever intervening, except when I told him about my doubts.
More than once I complained about the difficulty of carrying out the task without Lacan lending an ear. He was aware of both the human and the negative tendency to complain and proceeded like the Zen master, who may simply not act or may even kick his disciple to change his position.
The translation took place over nine months, the symbolic time of a pregnancy. I was also going to speak about this before the end of the analysis.

To quell my nostalgia for Brazil, I did what other Latin Americans living in Paris did. They used tampered telephone booths in order to talk for a long time without paying. As soon as one booth was repaired, someone in the group was messing with another one. It was theft, of course, but this never occurred to anyone. None of us would have cared anyway. In the 1970s, young people claiming to be on the Left valued thieving, an attitude justified by the logic of TQPB, *Tout ce Qui peut porter Préjudice à la Bourgeoisie* (Anything that can harm the Bourgeoisie). Of course, I did not say a word about this in the analysis.

One day, after having searched for a long time, I found an unrestricted booth at Saint-Germain-des-Prés. I chatted with my friends from across the Atlantic and would have been very happy if I had not realized that I no longer had my pendant, the eternal glass eye. I spent most of the night scanning the streets, walking down Boulevard Saint-Germain, retracing my steps, down Boulevard Saint-Michel to the Seine. I suddenly felt extremely vulnerable. In fact, I was in a state of hopelessness.

I fell asleep at dawn and almost missed the session the next day.

"Tell me."
"I have nothing to say. I lost my eye."
"What? Your eye?"
"Yes, my glass eye. Without it, I can't stay here."

Without hesitation, the Doctor told me that I had to get another one right away.

"What do you mean?"
"Send a message to Brazil! Make the call!"

I left the session completely bewildered. How was it that the Doctor, a psychoanalyst by profession, supported my belief in this fetish? Obviously, the priority was to avoid the rupture—*primo non rompere*. If respecting my belief was the condition for me to stay, he could only agree. The Doctor was not there to oppose me, but to be my analyst and remain so. He knew very well that the analysand's resistance finds a thousand and one pretexts to manifest itself.

I learned from this session that the analyst must be attuned to the analysand in order to avoid the resistance that always threatens the analytic process. Analysis sparks discoveries and it can be difficult to endure their effects.

To remain in tune with me, Lacan was able to say what a saint's father would have said. He was an actor pretending not to act and slipped into every role that was imposed on him. For the sole purpose of maintaining the transference with me, he became Brazilian. He surely did this with other analysands coming from other horizons. For him, the only nationality that was worthwhile was analysis. Dogmatism had no place. At 5, rue de Lille, Lacan's practice was guided by learned *ignorance*.

My attachment to the glass eye had to do with childhood. I was raised by my parents in the Catholic religion, but my nanny's world was one of religious syncretism where Christian faith and African beliefs intermingled. The glass eye symbolized my entire past. I could not live without it in Paris or elsewhere. I followed Lacan's advice and ordered another one.

So, I authorized myself to be like an aunt who, to the despair of her Maronite family, resorted to spiritualism after the death of her son. I told this story to the Doctor.

> "My cousin died at the seaside; his head hit a rock while diving. His father went to identify the body at the morgue and my aunt collapsed at the funeral. Then she gave herself up to a psychic medium."
>
> "Hmm …"
>
> "Everyone despised her for having gone over to spiritualism. The family stuck to its everlasting *Maktub*."
>
> "What else?"
>
> "My grandparents had emigrated because of religious intolerance yet they mocked my aunt and her adherence to spiritualism. For her, it was the only way to find her son and to talk with him. How can one be a victim of intolerance and become intolerant?"

Lacan left me with this question, recognizing that the important thing was for me to find an answer. This occurred when I understood that it was possible to identify with the torturer by reading *The Story of O*. Not content to submit to all the violence inflicted by her lover, O understood it as an honor.

On the one hand, Lacan did not waste time. He interrupted the session as soon as it was necessary. This was his way of opening the path for each person to become who they are.

In my case, this meant not only accepting my olive skin color but also accepting a body that did not fit French fashion. These were futile preoccupations, certainly, but I dared to speak about them.

> "I like to attend fashion shows. But I would be unable to wear the clothes of the great designers. I would have to lose at least ten kilos …"

"Hmm ..."

"And that's not all ... From the waist up, I wear a size 42, from the waist down a size 46."

"Fashion is not for everyone ..."

"It is not made for a Hottentot Venus ..."

"Hottentot?"

"My body is disproportionate, like hers ... it is the tradition in my country."

"Which country? Can you tell me?"

With that, he closed the session. I left as upset as I was intrigued. How could he ask me such a question? Where did this doubt come from? Lacan already knew that, apart from Brazil, I had been shaped by Lebanon and by France. Perhaps he wanted me to settle in France permanently, practice psychoanalysis, and translate his work. Perhaps he had used doubt to counter the dogmatism of my certainty.

It must be said that Brazil was more my country than the others: it was in its language that I dreamed, that I wrote. Even then, I needed writing to fill my life. One of the reasons for my transference to Lacan was certainly his poetic relationship to language. He took advantage of it to create neologisms and make puns, as is customary in Brazil.

Lacan's doubt had upset me. But that night I had a curious dream in which he appeared brandishing a baton. He said *piano, piano,* and then *l-pi-l-a-l-no,* putting the letter *l* before each syllable as children do.

When I woke up, I associated the *l* with Lebanon and my childhood, which I had spent in a small town in the interior of Brazil. There my ancestors lived between their shop, their house, and their garden. It was a small town that was a bit like the Lebanon of Brazil and to which, as an adult, I never returned. It was the analysis that made me return to this vital space.

My ancestors had settled in two streets that formed an L shape. We, the children, would go from one house to the other to play and gorge ourselves on dried fruits and Eastern specialties prepared by my grandmother and my aunts with vegetables from the garden. The day consisted of sweets and bedtime was the only inconvenience.

During the sessions, I had never been able to talk about my childhood. After this dream, I realized how much it meant to me. You can forget your childhood, but it does not forget you. My paternal grandfather dreamed of the bleating of the goats that existed in his native mountain and my grandmother always mentioned "the water from the spring there."

After Lacan's question about my true country, I skipped the session. I probably could not bear the doubt, which had driven me away from him or which, technically speaking, had caused a *negative transference*.

More than once, I had missed the scheduled session without paying for it. By doing so, I was not keeping my word. Why was this? Did I want to make sure that the Doctor had missed me?

I no longer remember what I said to Lacan during the session that followed. I know that after speaking and settling the fee, his reaction surprised me.

"What is this you are giving me?"
"For the session, of course."
"Then give me double."
"What do you mean?"
"Yes, double."
"That's not possible."
"It has to be."

Having no other option, I complied. Why was he demanding payment only now, when I had failed to pay for other sessions that I had not attended without warning? Where was the logic? What could it mean? On the quays, I remembered a theft that I had committed in primary school.

The English teacher used American chalk—which came in all colors—and I wanted it, too. One day, while she was away, I stuffed the chalk in my schoolbag and took off. The next day at recess, the teacher allowed everyone but me to leave the classroom without explaining why. He left me alone with my conscience.

Like my teacher, the Doctor led me to decipher the motive of my conduct. In fact, I owed him for many sessions. If he had asked me to settle everything, he would have collected the actual debt. By asking me for double, he recovered a symbolic debt, the one I owed on my word. It was not a question of rectifying a situation, but of making me understand that I was at fault vis-à-vis the law.

I understood why he had asked me for double. What I did not understand was the pleasure I felt in not paying for the session or for the phone calls to Brazil. How do you explain this taste for transgression? I discovered it when I remembered a story about my immigrant ancestors.

Knowing that brocade was not available in Brazil, they had taken the precious piece of cloth from Lebanon, wrapped it around their bodies, and sold it on arrival. This was strictly forbidden, but they boasted that they had fooled the customs officer: "The clerk didn't register our name properly, but we got him!"

This apologetics for transgression engendered the desire to transgress in their descendants. I had been the object of such a desire more than once, a deviation with which the Doctor no longer wanted to comply.

It was after this "double" session that the theme of motherhood arose in the analysis, again through a dream. I appeared with ten men who courted me by offering fruit. We were all up in the clouds. I began the session by recounting this story. Then I continued.

"There were eleven of us in all, like a soccer team."
"Curious."
"I woke up thinking I wanted to be in Brazil."
"That's obvious."
"What is less obvious is the fantasy I had ..."
"Tell me."
"The fantasy of having enough kids to form a soccer team with them, ten kids."
"What else?"
"I don't know ... I dreamed of ten kids, when I can't even have one."
"You can't?"
"I can't imagine the father of the child."
"That's it. See you tomorrow."

No interruption was more significant. The impossibility of imagining the father had to do with the desire to give my name to the child. It was impossible to let someone else do it for me, to accept the condition imposed on the female sex: conceiving without being able to name.

My conflicting relationship with the female sex was explained by my family history. As the eldest child in a family of Lebanese origin, I should have been born male, not female. When my mother gave birth to me, my maternal grandfather had this to say: "Nice child. Too bad it's a girl ..." This was Brazil in 1944. In 1961, in England, the future Princess of Wales, Diana, was the victim of a similar disdain. Her father announced her birth without mentioning the sex, saying only that she was a "perfect specimen of the human race." There are phrases and omissions that are enough to dig someone else's grave.

Fortunately, my father educated me to be able to exercise the same skills as a man. He accompanied me in my studies and sports ... *mens sana in corpore sano.* Yet being the firstborn child complicated my life terribly. In the imaginary of the extended family, birthright was destined for the male sex. Unconsciously, so as to be loved, I wanted to live up to the family's expectations. Pregnancy would make my biological sex evident and become a hindrance for me. Without denying my femininity, I leaned towards a certain undefined sexuality.

Motherhood in my case was not natural. I had to conquer it in spite of myself. This theme came back with insistence in the analysis. After my mother's lullaby, it manifested itself through another dream.

Somewhere, I am waiting for the bus with a pregnant friend. Then I am in another place, which I do not recognize. Looking at the people around me, I realize that I am at home in my city, but the streets are narrow like those of the medieval cities of Europe. A stranger chases me. Despite the stifling heat, he is wearing a suit and a bow tie ... Suddenly, he shouts that the police are looking for me. My friend calls him a swindler and I am ready to turn myself in. A policeman appears, I brandish my diploma and say to him: "Do you think I'm an outsider?"

I admit to the Doctor that I don't understand why the policeman is chasing me.

"What crime have I committed?"
"Tell me."
"The friend in the dream is pregnant. The crime has something to do with that ..."
"Hmm ..."
"I'm at home in my country, the stranger in the suit is the father ... He wears a bow, he can only be a Frenchman. The pregnancy ... the father ... a French father ..."

I would have remained silent for a long time if the Doctor had not spoken.

"What else?"
"I don't know ... a Franco-Brazilian child ... How I wish I had one."
"And why not?"

The Doctor had said that I could invent a lullaby for my child. With his question, he was now bringing motherhood into the realm of possibility. This was because my desire to be a mother had been clearly expressed. This desire went against the fantasy of being a man, which was categorically imposed on me. In other words, he radically shook up my imaginary, pushing me into a new position. Of course, it is thanks to a manifestation of the unconscious, during the analysis, that such a change could occur. This gives full meaning to the *subversion of desire*, a concept so dear to Lacan.

But how could I see myself in the role of a mother, when I could not identify with my ancestors, women educated only for the prospect of marriage and conception? One of my aunts demanded a male child from her womb to feel legitimate. There were novenas upon novenas— devotional prayers upon devotional prayers—to conceive the little prince in addition to promises, such as, for instance, that in exchange for heaven granting her the blessing of conceiving a boy, she was ready to crawl across the city on her knees.

Without the comfort of identification with my ancestors, my mother's behavior made me fragile. Throughout my childhood, she would rush to console me at the slightest cry, teaching me impatience and fostering my dependence. How could I not see myself as weak and vulnerable? Due to this other fantasy, pregnancy seemed out of reach.

Yet we are more than just our imaginary, and analysis exists precisely so that we can reinvent ourselves. The session where I talked about my fantasy of fragility allowed me to access a new consciousness.

My mother never imagined her existence outside of mine. She always made a point of taking me to school herself, and she picked me up every day. When I was eighteen and took the entrance exam to medical school, she wanted to accompany me to the examination room. When I graduated, I left home. But she would take care of any place that I settled in …

Silence.

"If I had a child, I would stop being her eternal daughter …"
"That's true."
"But what is the use to say the truth?"
"What else?"

"Always the same question ..."

"Hmm ..."

"I don't know with what strength ..."

"Yes, tell me ..."

"I don't know how my body could conceive a child ... if it would bear it."

There and then, the doctor interrupted the session and I remembered my mother's story. Before giving birth to me, she had conceived a boy who had been strangled in utero with the umbilical cord. This tragedy explained her overprotectiveness toward me.

My mother never let me do anything in the home or in the family business. Before he died, my father had secured our future. Mom took over the management of the business and encouraged her three daughters to continue their education.

This is why I was so profoundly negligent with regard to all that has to do with money. Thus, I did not always slip what was needed into my wallet before going to the session. One day, it was in the waiting room that I realized it.

The Doctor called me and I walked in with my empty wallet in hand.

"What's that in your hand?"

"This? It's an oversight. Today, I can't tell you anything."

"How come?"

"I forgot to go to the bank and I came to you with nothing."

"So, go to the bank and come back tomorrow."

The Doctor sent me to the bank because he listened to my *I can't tell you anything*. As I did not allow myself to speak without paying, he took me at my word to pull me out from my negligence. This was also a way to get me out of the maternal tutelage.

Even if at first the sessions seemed meaningless, everything followed a logic for Lacan that could be deduced from a discourse in the process of being constructed. Through tireless practice, he had developed the sharpest listening ability, which fully justified the use of the short session.

It was not without ulterior motives that the Doctor had sent me to the bank. The question of money was central to the story of a poor family that had left the Middle East without a penny, a family that had fought hard to make a place for itself in the sun through the humiliation of peddling. My paternal grandmother was the only one who ironized those who had the illusion of getting rich quickly in America. The others remained in denial of their origins, and I was raised as if we had always had personal wealth. Everything around me was done to forget the tragic past of immigration.

Already, at our first meeting, Lacan had shown that he was curious about my origins and this was not by chance. For him, the analytic treatment was an epic and the analysand was a hero. Thanks to his listening, he made each session a surprising event, even *extraordinary* in the literal sense of the word. He gave the treatment a subjective epic dimension that it had not had before. It was an approach similar to that of Freud. By comparing neurotics to Oedipus and Hamlet, he made them heroes of tragedy, when during the same era they were treated only with drugs or locked up in asylums. This epic conception of the treatment is one of the many examples of Lacan's return to Freud.

The desire to be a mother was insistent in my dreams.

"I dreamt of my country again … of an African ritual held on an island in Bahia."
"I'm listening."
"There's no need to talk about it, you won't understand anything."
"Are you sure?"
"Let's say that you will hardly understand anything."
"Go ahead then."
"This religion only exists in Africa and Brazil. The ritual I attended makes the ancestors of the people in the village visible. They are the Egun or the Baba Egun; they have the power to heal."
"The power to heal …"
Yes … the Egun suddenly appears to the sound of drums in the middle of the ritual. He is dressed in strips of velvet and silk sewn with mirrors, bells, shells, and various emblems. These strips of fabric are attached to a kind of hood. One cannot see his face as it is covered with a net. The Egun stands on a throne to speak. He tells those who complain to him of pain or illness what they should do. His voice is hoarse and hollow …

Silence.

"In my dream, I am sitting in front of the throne. The Egun beckons
    me to come closer. Despite my fear, I get up and go toward him.
    Suddenly the word *Seriema* resounds in the space."
"What does this word mean?"
"Seriema is the name of a bird in Tupi-Guarani."
"Hmm ..."
"When I am in front of the Egun, he says *Seriema, ema, emi* ..."
"How?"
"*Seriema, ema, emi.*"

Silence.

"And then?"
"I don't know."
"No, really?"
"Emi ... my Lebanese grandmother called me *emi* ... It means *mother*
    in Arabic ..."

The Doctor immediately interrupted the session. Thanks to what the
Egun had told me and to free association, the word *mother*, the magic
word, had entered the scene in the language of the forgotten lullaby. It
was a new manifestation of my desire to have a child. There was nothing
more to say.

Lacan knew that the unconscious can manifest itself in any language,
one of his ways of thwarting censorship. This session testifies to this,
as did the one in which the unnamable name of the father—Rachid—
re-emerged through a French word *rat*. When the door is closed, the
unconscious comes out through the window.

Moreover, Lacan knew how important Arabic was to me. It was the
hidden language, the one in which my ancestors spoke among themselves
about what we were forbidden to know. Arabic was deliberately not
transmitted to us. In their imagination, this language could no longer
be of any use to us. Furthermore, due to the xenophobic environment,
it could be troublesome. For them, it was as if the integration of the
descendants implied the rejection of their native language.

The prospect of motherhood tormented me. Not because I demanded a male child from my womb, but because the devotion of my ancestors to their families was not compatible with what was happening in the 1970s. Without being a militant feminist, I knew that I belonged somewhere at work, not in the domestic scene. On the other hand, every time I thought about my mother's story, pregnancy frightened me. It was as if the saga of the stillborn child was bound to repeat.

It was when my mother came to France to see me that the desire to separate myself from her, or rather from her past, manifested itself in a dramatic way. The day after she arrived, I had a new dream.

I am in the desert, aimless, and completely lost. Suddenly, she comes toward me, calling me daughter. With each step forward that my mother takes, I take one step back. Then she gives me an injection and the word *spirochaeta pallida* is written on the sand.

"The syphilis bacteria …"
"Yes, but why?"
"Tell me, I'm listening."
"My mother chasing me … *spirochaeta pallida*, the germ that drives
    you crazy."
"What else?"
"I don't know … my mother, she pursues me … the stillborn child.
    I wanted to go crazy to escape her, to escape the impossibility of
    giving birth. I can't take it anymore."

Repeating that I was going to go crazy, I broke down in tears. Lacan intervened in a categorical tone.

"Nobody becomes crazy because they want to!"

My desire for madness did not mean I was going to attain it. Lacan knew the perils of the analytical process and, without making any concessions, knew how to find the words so that the analysand could bear the manifestations of the unconscious. In this situation, he was able to tell me what I needed to hear. Gradually, I stopped crying.

The session produced effects over the next few days. I remembered an aunt of mine who was said to be a bit strange and ended up in a psychiatric institution. I liked her very much for her extravagance, which probably caused her to be committed. Arab women of her generation were expected to be totally self-effacing, and at the slightest deviation, they were accused of being crazy.

In a different register, I suffered because of the archaism of my family. On the one hand, I had been brought up to be an independent professional. On the other hand, I did not have freedom as a woman. I had to behave like the girls of the previous generation, and since I did not fit into this mold, the relationship with my parents was conflicted. This was especially the case with my father, who was possessively jealous, forbidding me to associate with other men. His attachment to was so intrusive that I was not able to be myself. He terrorized me to the point of making me an orphan before my time.

So many years later, I did not imagine that my fear of intrusion would resurface during a session that could have been the last one, without Lacan's tactfulness. After half an hour in the waiting room, the Doctor brought me into the office. I lay down on the couch, as usual. But he did not sit in his chair. He walked over to the couch and just stood there looking at me.

"What gives you the right to stand there"?

The question was phrased so abruptly that he went to sit in his chair and repeated my words.

"By what right?"
"Yes, that's what I said."

The Doctor remained silent, no doubt sensing that I was dealing with a threat from the past.

"If you were attracted to me, I would have to leave."

With that, the session ended, and I left in silence, astonished by the violence of my words. The interruption also had the function of provoking such astonishment. In the following days, I remembered my adolescence, including the scenes caused by my father's jealousy toward me. He went so far as to hang a whip on the wall of the entrance so that I would not forget to not go out without permission and that I would respect the established curfew. Nevertheless, I always found a way to get around his prohibitions.

I never expected the Doctor to approach. He appeared to me as the threatening father and I demanded that he stay away. I was no longer grappling with the name of the father, but with the father's passion and my Oedipus complex, which was instrumental in my choice of Lacan as my analyst. But I would only discover this at the very end of the analysis, which would coincide with my return to Brazil.

Lacan had notified me that he would not be working the following week, but a few days later, he called me.

"So, when are you coming?"

I was so surprised that I did not know what to say.

"Well?"
"You suspended the sessions, so I have decided to leave Paris. My bags are packed. I need to take some time to reread the translation of your *Freud's Writings on Technique* one last time. I'll be back next Monday."
"Well, my dear, see you on Monday."

When I returned, I printed a copy of the text and brought it to the session. I put the large manuscript on Lacan's desk and lay down on the couch. Contrary to my expectation, he simply said that it was not his language and sat back in his chair.

How could he show such indifference, when I had made a great effort to translate his text and he had always been willing to lift all my doubts? This was the first of his seminars translated into Portuguese. I felt deeply frustrated and could not help but tell him.

"You don't care much about your analysands ... I've even been told that in your files we are all categorized according to a diagnosis."
"What are you saying?"
"Yes, yes ... catalogued as hysterical, obsessive, perverse ...
"I also know what yours is."

Lacan responded to the provocation, but ignored my complaint. He knew that time was precious and was not there to waste it. Moreover, his indifference to the manuscript and its language made it clear to me that this translation business was mine. It could not be otherwise, since emigration imposes the passage from one language to another.

My Lebanese grandfather used to tell me that, although he was poor, he felt rich having learned five words in Portuguese: *pernilongo, pão, leite, água, obrigado*—mosquito, bread, milk, water, thank you. Lacan was certainly very satisfied with my translation of his seminar, but that was not the point. Like all of the greats, he never left his role. Jean-Paul Belmondo did not give up acting on the day of his daughter's sudden death. His performance was impeccable, and I did not hear about the tragedy on the radio until I got home.

With the translation, I not only learned French; I also deepened my Portuguese. I was very tempted to write a satire about the impossibilities I had faced during the analysis. I talked about it during the session.

> "In Brazilian children's literature, there is a rag doll called Emilia. She makes fun of adults, says that they never learn anything, not even the simplest thing in the world: *make-believe.*"
> "And then?"
> "And then I'd like to write a fiction, to imagine ... to make a satire of what I have said here ... the difficulty of accepting my origins, the color of my skin, my sex ... an abyss of difficulties."
> "Hmm ..."
> "I always liked what Emilia said. It is while dreaming of her that I thought of writing a satire ... to laugh at it all."
> "You'll write it, maybe."

This time, Lacan maintained my desire with his *maybe.* Now that the translation was finished, I wanted to write directly in my own language, a step that would be decisive for returning to Brazil. To write or not to write depended on me and me alone.

However, it was not writing but the need to spread psychoanalytic theory that I invoked to justify my decision to leave. This justification earned me the title of *redemptress* by the Doctor. Was it because he knew how necessary psychoanalysis was in a country that had been built in the absence of a father figure and where the law was deprived of all force?

The word *redemptress* continued to resonate with its cohort of questions. Was the redemption of my country really my destiny? Or was I not called to remain in France? The question arose not only because of my attachment to the Doctor but also because I had met the man who would become my husband and the father of my son. Besides, it was very difficult to leave Paris and its beauty.

My doubts were multiplying, as my resident card was about to expire. I would not be able to stay in France legally for much longer. I felt unable to make the decision to go back to Brazil.

I left my house to go to the Doctor's. When I arrived at rue de Lille, I stayed there, walking around the neighborhood. Suddenly, I heard my name being shouted. It was an exuberant blonde.

"The Doctor wants a word with you."
"What?"

Lacan had spotted me and stopped his car, in the middle of traffic, just to talk with me. The blonde woman repeated what she had just told me, and I approached the car, rather embarrassed.

"You came all the way here and didn't go up? Come back tomorrow, same time."

I was resisting analysis, that was obvious, and Lacan had found a way to oppose my resistance. He, decidedly, was not resisting it. This episode illustrates the scope of the concept of the *resistance of the analyst*, which manifests itself when the analyst lets the analysand sabotage the work.

At the next session, I raised the issue of my residency card. I could only stay in France if my authorization was extended. Lacan did not hesitate to write to the police chief that same day.

> *I, the undersigned, declare that Mrs. Betty Milan has come from Brazil to follow the teaching provided by the Freudian School of Paris of which I am the director. This has been since November 1973. Given her assiduity, this teaching requires authorization for her—this is the reason for this letter—to extend her stay.*
>
> J. Lacan

The dice were thrown and I would stay for some time. Whenever I talked about going back to Brazil, the Doctor held me in the mesh of his net and the session ended with a *when will I see you?* or a *see you tomorrow*. The separation was difficult after all that had happened. If I had not conquered America, I had become certain that by practicing both writing and psychoanalysis, I was on the right track.

Shortly before the end of the analysis, I told the doctor that I needed to heal myself from having to heal. He only answered with *curious*. I remembered an analysand whom I always met at the same bar and who had up to several sessions a day with Lacan.

"How many times have you said *curious* to the analysand who is
always at the same bar and comes to see you at all hours of the
day? The analysis must have cost him the equivalent of a forest.
He passed all his property onto you."

"What else?"

"What else? I have nothing more to say."

"Yes ..."

"Yes what? You are not interested in what I say. Only in what there
is still to say."

"That's it. See you tomorrow."

Once again, Lacan turned a deaf ear to the provocation. He knew
perfectly well that the analysis was coming to an end and that at the
slightest misstep I would leave without having said the essential. Only
his intuition allowed me to arrive at my destination.

Neither my desire to return to Brazil nor the dissemination of his
psychoanalysis there had been able to convince the Doctor to let me
go. For my part, I only thought about living in my mother tongue, the
language of *ão*. It was a persistent desire that seemed to me to be an
unstoppable argument. Did Lacan not say that language is a treasure,
going so far as to introduce the concept of *lalangue*? He could therefore
perfectly understand that I wanted to live in mine.

Before the session, I took detours through the neighborhood.
The Doctor wore a velvet-and-silk-striped jacket and a pink shirt
reminiscent of the cotton candy sold at the entrance of circuses.

"Your shirt reminds me of a sweet that I ate as a child, at the circus ...
and also of another one that exists only in my country."

"What is it called?"

"*Pé de moleque.*"

"*Mo-lek ... ?*"

"It means smart kid. A sweet that all Brazilians know and that no
Frenchman can imagine. One more reason to go and live in my
country ..."

"Of course."

"You always agree, but you don't understand what I'm saying. I don't
want to live here anymore, I'll go away. No word in the French
language makes me dream. For me, French words are like objects:
I keep bumping into them. Portuguese words are translucent,
light as veils ... it's the veil I want."

"Well, my dear, see you tomorrow."

DOCTEUR JACQUES LACAN

ANCIEN CHEF DE CLINIQUE À LA FACULTÉ

5, RUE DE LILLE, VII*

260-72-93   SUR RENDEZ-VOUS

À la Préfecture de police

Je soussigné certifie que Madame Betty Milan est venue du Brésil pour suivre l'enseignement distribué par l'École freudienne de Paris dont je suis le directeur. Ceci depuis novembre 1973

Son assiduité à cet enseignement impose qu'on lui permette — c'est là l'objet de ce certificat — la prolongation de son séjour

Lacan

Ce 4. II - 77

Figure 2 Letter from Lacan (1977).

The Doctor got up, I settled the payment and left.

The word *veil* made me dream about my father and the odalisque—harem concubine—costume that I had worn several times as a child for the carnival. When I woke up, I did not understand what the odalisque was doing in my dream. Did it remind me of the Sultan? The Eastern origins of my father? Or his insane jealousy? He always wanted to keep me to himself: it was as if he was forcing me to wear a veil. Suddenly, everything became clear. I finally understood why I had taken on an analyst whose language was not my own. I needed someone in front of whom I could not reveal myself completely. Lacan did not know Portuguese, and he responded perfectly to this imperative. Despite myself, I had not ceased to be the object of the father's desire. Paradoxically, I had not chosen Lacan for what he knew, but for what he did not know, what he could not even be brought to know.

Lacan had suggested from the first session of the second stage that I go and do an analysis with a Portuguese woman. He had had the intuition that the question of language was fundamental. But he accepted that I rejected his suggestion in order to avoid a rupture and to allow me to make the journey.

After the dream, I bought my ticket to Brazil. I only intended to come back to 5, rue de Lille for a supervisory meeting (*contrôle*). Would Lacan agree to this?

"Of course, my sister."
My sister … ! I could not believe my ears.

I went to the supervision to discuss the case of Miss Y., my analysand whose treatment was interrupted due to my forthcoming departure. Y. was an alcoholic, and I presented her a bottle of Châteauneuf-du-Pape for her last session. This was an aberrant act with regard to the rule of abstention: the analyst limits himself to interpreting, without any other form of intervention. My act could be justified, but I dreaded this supervisory meeting. What if I were expelled from the Freudian School of Psychoanalysis, as I had been from the Brazilian Society?

I began by telling Lacan that the rule of abstention—like all the others—had to be considered in light of each particular case, and then I spoke about Y. The young woman had come to me because her previous analyst had kicked her out when she arrived to the session drunk.

Y. told me that she drank because she had trouble talking, establishing a direct link between talking and drinking. She was not addicted like alcoholics who have to leave the theater to drink in the middle of the movie, but she could empty a whole bottle, "drink until she was disgusted."

Her mother, a doctor, only believed in medication and her father kept telling her to shut up. She was afraid I would do the same. What Y. wanted most was to be able to talk without drinking.

She was caught in a vice, between the father's imperative to *keep quiet*, which made her swallow every word, and the drink, which widely opened the valve of speech. By drinking, Y. could speak without disobeying the father—since it was not her, but the drunk woman who spoke. How and when would she cease to be the object of the father's desire to become the subject of her own desire?

One day, Y. told me that as a child, she used to eat everything in the refrigerator. It occurred to me that she might be able to free herself from alcoholism if she was able to savor instead of swallowing. On our next-to-last appointment, I was surprised when she told me that she had a dream about me ... I was offering her a bottle of fine wine, "a great Brazilian brand." The desire expressed in the dream confirmed my hypothesis.

Tasting is not drinking. I had the opportunity to observe this in the cellars of France. The true taster tries the wine and spits it out, before describing its appearance, its aroma, its flavor ... Tasting and talking are inseparable, so, it was reasonable to imagine that, through savoring, Y. would leave her position and finally manage to talk without drinking. Hence my idea to offer her an excellent Châteauneuf-du-Pape at her last session with me. It was with this enigmatic gift that I parted with her, hoping that she would try to decipher it, and that, if necessary, she would go to a third analyst.

I was not expelled from the Freudian School of Paris for breaking the rule of abstention. My act was aberrant from this point of view, but not from the point of view of analytic theory, which awaits its renewal within practice. Y. told me later that from the Châteauneuf session onwards, she had stopped getting drunk.

"You've got the bottle ..."

It was with this play on words that the Doctor said goodbye to me after the supervisory meeting. In French, "*avoir la bouteille*" is a colloquial expression that means that a person has gained experience or wisdom. He therefore gave me what I needed: the recognition of the ability to practice psychoanalysis wherever I wanted.

More than forty years have passed, but it is as if it were yesterday, because 5, rue de Lille does not cease to be present. It was there that resistance to desire could be overcome, freedom acquired, life reinvented. The Doctor did not accept time being squandered, but always gave his time to those who were really ready for analysis. Yes, it was worth crossing the ocean "*as if to discover America*" to find my path. I am one of those who had the privilege of having believed in Lacan.

GOODBYE DOCTOR
(A Play)

Translated by Clifford E. Landers

to the memory of Oswald de Andrade
and
for José Celso Martinez Corrêa

DESCRIPTION

In the third generation of a family of Lebanese immigrants in Brazil, Seriema lives the drama of a Western descendant of a people from the Middle East. Her ancestors needed to sire a male firstborn to meet the expectations of the family. Instead, she was born. Pregnancy becomes a problem for Seriema who, following two miscarriages, and contrary to her wishes, separates from her husband. Why is motherhood impossible for her? Is it because she cannot identify with the women in her family or some other reason?

Seriema decides to leave Brazil in order to forget the drama of separation. She wins a grant and goes to France, where she begins an analysis. Through it, she discovers the true reason why she cannot give birth, namely her unconscious desire to satisfy the will of her father, who never authorized her to conceive. Thanks to listening to the analyst, Seriema ceases to be the victim of her unconscious and grasps the possibility of choosing a father for her child and thus becoming a mother.

The play is structured around the analytic sessions. The way each session ends is always a function of what is said during it, and the text clearly indicates this. The Doctor, by interrupting the session to interpret the analysand's words, underscores the essential elements of what she has said. Each session is one scene; given the nationality of the analysand, the transition from one scene to another can be punctuated by a drumbeat.

CHARACTERS

Seriema: the Brazilian analysand

The Doctor: a French analyst

Maria: Seriema's nanny

In addition to the two characters, a dancer for the role of Maria, Seriema's nanny, who appears in two scenes, dancing, and whose voice is heard offstage.

ACT I

SCENE 1

(Paris. The Doctor's office, with a window and two doors in the rear. Analysands enter through the door on the left and exit through the door on the right. On the left side of the office, two velvet armchairs. Between them, a small table with telephone. On the right side, the couch and armchair of the analyst, imposing.
The Doctor and Seriema are seated in the chairs, facing each other. The Doctor is wearing a blazer and a white shirt, without a tie. Seriema is in a suit, long pants and a coat, carrying a masculine leather purse. As the play goes on, the heroine's clothing becomes progressively more feminine.)

DOCTOR
But why did you separate? To this day I don't know the reason, the real reason.

SERIEMA
I didn't want the separation. It was Antonio who moved out. After the second miscarriage.

DOCTOR
There were two miscarriages.

SERIEMA
Yes. I lost a child twice. The second time, Antonio went crazy. He smashed everything in the house and disappeared. He asked a friend to come get what he needed, but he wouldn't send any message. *(Pause)* I wanted him back. I waited for three months—nothing. I did everything possible to obtain a scholarship. I got it and packed my bags. I went far away, hoping he would change his mind. So far, nothing. *(Pause)* I need to find out why I'm alone ... why I lost Antonio.

DOCTOR
You didn't separate, you lost Antonio.

SERIEMA
(Pause) I also lost Brazil ... I didn't know what it means to be a foreigner. *(Sarcastically)* "Where are you from? What country?" And I never know if I'm speaking correctly. For the least little action in the past, French uses three words. *(Pronouncing the words in French one by one)* For "he ate," *il a mangé.* For the simple number ninety, three words: *quatre vingt dix.* Here, I'm constantly translating from one language to the other; I'm forced

to *think* all the time. In Brazil, the language thinks for me ...
Even having a Coke is complicated here. If you don't say *cocaaa*
instead of *coca*, and if you don't change the indefinite article and
say *un coca* instead of *une coca*, nobody understands.

DOCTOR
Hmm. What else? Go on.

SERIEMA
I don't know ...

DOCTOR
(Soliloquy) "I don't know." She wants and doesn't want to do
analysis. If the analyst isn't resourceful he's lost. When he's
attacked, he has to keep quiet. If he doesn't, the analysis is over
before it begins. *(Pause)* And is she going to go on like that, in
silence? She's pretty ... straight dark hair ... Could she have
some Indian ancestry? *(Addressing Seriema)* Is there Indian
blood in your family?

SERIEMA
(Soliloquy) What? Me, an Indian? That's all I need. What is
he thinking? That I'm the descendant of those Indians who
ran around naked and threw themselves onto European ships
believing they were headed to heaven? *(Sarcastically)* They were
supposed to exhibit their feathered headdress and brandish their
war club to liven up French festivals, risking death from a cold
or from diarrhea. Where's your bow and arrow, Seriema? Where
are the feathers and maracas?

DOCTOR
You need to tell me what goes through your mind. Is there
Indian blood in your family?

SERIEMA
Seriema is the Indian name of a Brazilian bird, a Tupi-Guarani
word. But there's nothing Indian in me. I've already mentioned
that I'm the granddaughter of people of Lebanese descent. My
grandmother emigrated to Brazil because her future husband
was there. An arranged marriage. And she didn't offer any
opposition. All she could say was, "From Lebanon to Brazil,
at fourteen, five children, because *maktub*, it was written, and
that is everything." *Maktub* and she boarded the ship, *maktub*

and she got married, *maktub* … It never entered her head that a woman could be free, have the same rights as a man.

DOCTOR
And what does your grandmother's story have to do with your own?

SERIEMA
When I was born, she said, "A lovely child. What a pity it's a girl." My birth was a disappointment; she wanted a male, a real firstborn. *What a pity it's a girl.* How can anyone say something like that? One sentence is enough to save or condemn a person, to dig a grave.

DOCTOR
True.

SERIEMA
And what about my aunt? She prayed day and night to conceive a male. "Hail Mary, full of grace, the Lord is with you … Hail Mary, full of grace, blessèd is the fruit—" She even promised to cross the city on her knees. Novenas and more novenas. *(Indignant)* Her entire pregnancy begging heaven for a son.

DOCTOR
Irrationality …

SERIEMA
An abomination!

DOCTOR
(Soliloquy) Pregnancy was torture in her family. Either the woman gave birth to a firstborn male or she was looked down upon. As if the sex of the child depended on the mother! The woman was treated unjustly merely for being a woman. *(Addressing Seriema)* Is there any relation between your story and that of your mother, or your aunt? I'm referring to the miscarriage … to the miscarriages.

SERIEMA
The doctor said it was a problem in the uterus …

DOCTOR
And you didn't know?

SERIEMA
Not the first time I lost the child, no.

DOCTOR
(*Surprised*) And later?

SERIEMA
I thought the problem wasn't anything serious and wouldn't have greater consequences. I only had an operation after the second miscarriage, when I was forced to … an infection and hemorrhaging … I could have died.

DOCTOR
(*Sighs*) You knew and didn't get treatment? (*Seriema lowers her head and remains silent*) Speak, I'm listening.

SERIEMA
I know it's my fault.

DOCTOR
You're responsible, not at fault. It wasn't a deliberate act. You didn't willfully ignore the problem.

SERIEMA
And so? Does it do any good to talk? Any good to lock the house after it's been robbed?

DOCTOR
There's no reason for despair. You're in analysis … You can set out on a new path, reinvent your own history. (*The Doctor stands up*)

SERIEMA
It's over? Already?

DOCTOR
Come back tomorrow.

SERIEMA
Tomorrow I can't.

DOCTOR
Then day after tomorrow, at five. (*The Doctor rises, as does Seriema. She puts the money on the table and leaves*) The miscarriage could have been avoided if she had listened to the doctor. She both wants to have a child and for some reason

doesn't want to. I hope she reflects on what she said, on the fact of not having gotten treatment, on ignoring what she knew, the "problem." The passion of ignorance is the worst passion of all. *(A pause. He sits down, picks up the telephone, and calls his secretary)* Get me Edouard, please. *(Irritated)* Of course Dr. Edouard. *(He waits)* Hello. Everything all right? Are the test results back yet? *(Pause)* Metastasis? More chemotherapy? *(He puts down the phone, disturbed, takes a deep breath, then resumes the conversation)* My mother won't do it. *(Pause)* It's going to be very difficult to persuade her … She keeps saying that she has lived long enough, and if it has metathesized she doesn't want further treatment … But I'll get back to you … *(Hangs up)* My God! My mother is condemned! I can't believe it. I have to tell my sister. It won't be easy. They're so close!

(The lights go out and come back on when the next scene begins. This should be repeated throughout the play)

SCENE 2

(Semidarkness. Maria speaks offstage to the sound of a distant drum. Meanwhile, the Doctor and Seriema remain motionless in the armchairs)

MARIA'S VOICE (offstage)
The cloud passes, and sadness too. Where are you, Seriema? You with your smile and your happiness. So far away! The cloud passes, and sadness too. Your husband left, but he can return. Call upon the Lady of Magic, the Goddess of Seduction, who can do everything. Call upon the incendiary angel. *(Tone of invocation)* O lady of the corolla of fire, prepare your magical potion—eye of salamander, toe of newt, tongue of dog—prepare it and have Antonio drink of it. Plunge into his heart the incandescent rod of passion. Invoke, Seriema. *(Same tone as at the beginning)* The wave comes and the wave goes. Maria waits for you, your Maria. Come back and hear the fiery beating of the drums. Come back and see the flight of birds ecstatic from the rhythm and the blue of the sky. The wave comes and the wave goes. *Volta Seriema. Você é filha da terra. A onda vai e a onda vem. Volta.*
(Office lighting)

SERIEMA
I dreamed about Maria, the Bahian woman who raised me …
Come back, she told me.

DOCTOR
(Pause) Nothing else?

SERIEMA
She advised me to call upon the Goddess of Seduction and ask her to bring back my husband. Unfortunately, I don't believe in magic. If I did, I wouldn't be here.

DOCTOR
And what else?

SERIEMA
(Pause) I've thought about what you said. You'd like me to have Indian blood … *(Laughs)* Then you could tell your fellow analysts that you analyzed a savage. *(Ironically)* The French love the noble savage.

DOCTOR
(Soliloquy) Why is she trying to provoke me? What does she gain? It would have been better if she'd thought about what

she said: *"I knew and didn't get treatment."* That's the reason for the separation. But it does no good to insist; forcing the issue only increases resistance … That's not why I'm here. Be patient, Doctor! *(Addressing her)* I'm listening.

SERIEMA
Actually, I would *like* to have Indian ancestors, Indian and Portuguese … And not be the descendant of immigrants.

DOCTOR
Why so?

SERIEMA
When I was a child, they called me "Turk." It was derogatory. Besides being illogical, because my grandfather left Lebanon to escape the Turks … to avoid having to serve in the occupying army.

DOCTOR
The Ottoman army.

SERIEMA
And my grandfather's name was changed when he got to Brazil … at customs. What did the name of an immigrant matter? Of a nobody? Later, as if that weren't enough, the nobody was called "people eater."

DOCTOR
(Surprised) People eater?

SERIEMA
Yes. My grandfather was an itinerant peddler. He sold merchandise in the small towns … A hundred-kilo sack on his back, from sunup to sundown. He would go from here to there, without lunch, without anywhere to sleep. "Cotton, silk, taffeta."

GRANDFATHER'S VOICE OFFSTAGE

Ahlo sahla! Algodão, seda, taffeta/Agulha, linha e tesoura pra corta/ Pente, caneta e papel/ Serve a moça e o Rafael Ahlo sahla! Cotton, silk, taffeta/ Needles, thread, and scissors to use/ Combs, paper, pens/ Prices so low you can't refuse.

He would greet people with *Ahlo sahla* and they would yell: "The Turk, the people eater is here!" Mothers would grab their children and run away. As if my grandfather were a cannibal. *People eater*, just because he spoke another language.

DOCTOR
And now you're in a country whose language isn't your own …
French isn't your mother tongue.

SERIEMA
That's true, but my grandparents are Lebanese immigrants. To
them, France was synonymous with civilization. My mother's
dream was to speak French. "Music to my ears," she used to say.
And I studied the language.

DOCTOR
Be that as it may, your mother tongue is Portuguese …

SERIEMA
So?

DOCTOR
You could do analysis with a Portuguese woman who lives here …

SERIEMA
(*Soliloquy*) A Portuguese, out of the question! Doesn't he know
that their language isn't the same? It seems to be, but it isn't.
The language of Portugal is one thing, the language of Brazil
is another. For sandwich, they say *prego*, which means nail. If
someone sees me eating a sandwich, they'll say I'm eating a
nail. *Broche*, which is brooch, in Portugal means fellatio. If I
compliment her on her brooch, she'll throw me out of her office.
No, it's impossible! From her point of view, I warp, I ruin the
language … I need Portuguese lessons more than sessions.

DOCTOR
So then?

SERIEMA
No, not with a Portuguese, no way! I'd rather not do an analysis.

DOCTOR
Well then, come back tomorrow. At five. (*The Doctor rises,
as does Seriema. She pays and leaves. The Doctor sits down*)
(*Soliloquy*) Seriema wants to do an analysis with me. And if not
with me, with no one. So it has to be the way she wants. But why
does she insist on doing her analysis in French, in a language
that's not her own? In any case, she knows what she wants and
doesn't want.

SCENE 3

(The Doctor is sitting alone in his office, reading a newspaper)

DOCTOR
(Looking at his watch) She may not come. She insists on doing
an analysis with me and then doesn't show up. I suggested
a Portuguese analyst; could it be that she feels rejected? Not
everything she says in Portuguese can be said in French. But
maybe that's not even the problem. Maybe it's the sex of the
analyst. It may be that she can't imagine doing an analysis
with a woman. *(Picks up the telephone. A pause)* Why doesn't
Mother answer? I asked my sister to stop by her house. *(Pause)*
Mother wants nothing to do with further chemotherapy. She has
suffered a lot, but I can't accept the idea. How can I live without
her? I want her to go on as long as possible. I know I'm selfish.
No one can ask another person to submit to treatment, however
much it hurts. I always told myself I would respect her decision,
but now … I'm not myself. *(He picks up the newspaper, turns the
pages, and reads a headline aloud)*

THE HEART HAS A GENDER

THE DIFFERENCES BETWEEN THE MALE AND FEMALE
HEARTS

Even in the anatomy of the heart, men and women are different!
(The telephone rings, he answers) Mother? Yes, I was the one who
called. *(Pause)* Of course, it's your life. I know, I know. You have
the right to decide. But— Mother? … Mother? Hello. Hello …
She hung up, shit! *(Replaces the phone on the hook and looks
at his watch again)* Five-thirty. Seriema isn't coming. *(He rises,
tosses away the newspaper, and leaves)*

SCENE 4

(The Doctor is standing. Seriema comes in, irritated. He sits down; she doesn't)

SERIEMA
(Standing) I heard you tell your secretary, "The little Brazilian woman can come in."

DOCTOR
Sit down. *(She sits but keeps her purse on her shoulder)* Yes, that's right. I said *little Brazilian*. In French the diminutive is affectionate.

SERIEMA
It reminded me of that "little Turk" from my childhood. I can't stand being labeled, Doctor. *("Doctor" is said sarcastically)*

DOCTOR
(Soliloquy) Shit! Why did I say *little Brazilian*?

SERIEMA
My grandfather told me that in Lebanon Christians were forced to wear a patch on their sleeve. They could only walk on one side of the street. Anyone walking on the other side would be arrested. "*Ishmel! Ishmel!* On the left." *(Irritated)* My grandfather was called a Christian, a Turk, and a people-eater, and now I'm the *little Brazilian woman*. I prefer to be called by my name: Seriema.

DOCTOR
For a good reason. And what else? Speak.

SERIEMA
I don't really know why I'm in France.

DOCTOR
(Soliloquy) She doesn't listen to herself, doesn't listen to what she says. *(Addressing Seriema)* You said that to your family France was synonymous with civilization—*(The phone rings. The Doctor checks the Caller ID screen and answers)* Yes, Mother. As soon as I'm finished, I'll call you. *(To Seriema)* Sorry.

SERIEMA
You can speak to her.

DOCTOR
No, I'm with you now.

SERIEMA
The truth is that my mother would have liked to be born here.
(Ironically) "Paris! The Eiffel Tower, the Pantheon, Edith Piaf,
the Rights of Man! The Sorbonne and real scholars. The City
of Light! Even the Statue of Liberty was sculpted in Paris!"
(A pause) But what do I have to do with my mother? I don't
know anyone here ... My room is tiny and the bed is so soft I
prefer sleeping on the floor. I grew up barefoot and now I never
take off my boots. I'm ten thousand kilometers from home.

DOCTOR
(Emphatically) It's true you left your country, your home, your
family ... It was a major dislocation. From one continent to another.

SERIEMA
Because of a husband who only wanted me if I could bear a
child. To him, no woman is unique. He has been "married"
several times. Any woman will do. I don't want to be put on a
pedestal, but I have no desire to be like all the others.

DOCTOR
(Soliloquy) An ancestor who needed to bring a male child into
the world in order to be loved ... She ran the risk of being
depreciated by giving birth. Seriema couldn't identity with
her, but she could have identified with some other woman and
undergone treatment to carry her pregnancy to term. Odd ... and
she always wears suits, with the same purse on her shoulder ...
She doesn't use jewelry, just that strange pendant. *(To Seriema)*
You said you don't want to be on a pedestal, but neither do you
want to be like all the others. What does that mean?

SERIEMA
What does it mean? I don't know.

DOCTOR
Think about it. That's all for today. *(He stands up and extends his
hand to receive his fee)* One hundred euros.

SERIEMA
Why a hundred?

DOCTOR
For today's session and the other one, the one you didn't show up for.

SERIEMA
I don't have a hundred … *(Looks in her wallet)* I do have a hundred.

DOCTOR
Excellent. *(Seriema, embarrassed, pays and leaves. The Doctor remains, seated)* Why does she say she doesn't have what she owes me when she has it?

SCENE 5

(Seriema is seated in one of the velvet armchairs. The Doctor is standing, staring at the pendant around her neck)

DOCTOR
What are you thinking?

SERIEMA
With you staring at me like that, I can't think. *(Soliloquy)* Should I say I don't like to be looked at that way? That his staring bothers me? That I don't want to be coveted by him? *(Addressing the Doctor)* You're the age my father would be if he were still alive.

DOCTOR
Hmm. *(The Doctor moves back a little, but remains standing)* What is it you have around your neck?

SERIEMA
The glass eye?

DOCTOR
Yes, the eye. Could it be a fetish?

SERIEMA
(Surprised) A fetish … The idea never occurred to me. *(Soliloquy)* After taking me for a savage, now he thinks I'm a fetishist …
(Silence)

DOCTOR
(The Doctor sits down) What else do you have to tell me?

SERIEMA
It's true that I only leave home wearing the eye, with my body "sealed."

DOCTOR
What?

SERIEMA
Sealed body means protected against envy … against the evil eye, as Maria says.

DOCTOR
Maria? Who is she?

SERIEMA

The black nanny who raised me … You don't listen. I've already mentioned her. Because she's the one I miss the most here. *(Semidarkness. The sound of a distant lullaby. Maria's voice offstage. Maria enters, dancing and singing a lullaby to little Seriema. Meanwhile, the Doctor and Seriema remain motionless)*

MARIA'S VOICE OFFSTAGE

Come here, my love, come here, my dear. Let me give you a hug. The little princess needs to go to sleep now. Afraid? Of what, my sweet girl? The howling wind? The lightning bolt? The thunder? While I am here? Sleep, my love, sleep. Come here, my love, come here, my dear. Let me give you a hug. The little princess needs to go to sleep now. *Medo? Ora … Do que? O vento que zuniu? O rato que caiu? O trovão? E eu aqui? Maria … Dorme, dorme.*
(Maria exits. Normal lighting of the analyst's office)

SERIEMA

Maria never left me. The eye is an amulet that she gave me, a talisman … I can't live without it.

DOCTOR

Can't live?

SERIEMA

No. But why do you ask?

DOCTOR

For you to become aware of your belief in magic.

SERIEMA

What?

DOCTOR

That's right, you believe in magic.

SERIEMA

(Ardently) I believe in Maria, who raised me. Maria is more than a mother, she's my protector … She gave me the talisman to protect me the way she is protected. Who doesn't need protection? Isn't it enough that I'm in France all alone? Living without love?

DOCTOR
Love … That's what you want more than anything.

SERIEMA
True. A man for whom I'm unique …

DOCTOR
As unique as a daughter can be to her father?

SERIEMA
(Pause) My father? He died years ago! I lost sight of him.

DOCTOR
(Soliloquy) She says she lost sight of her father. That kind of
forgetting is both strange and important. *(To Seriema)* Well, I'll
see you next time.

SERIEMA
(Ironically) Next time? What do you mean next time?

DOCTOR
*(The Doctor stands up. Seriema pays and leaves. Then he sits
down and makes notes. The phone rings. He looks at Caller ID
and answers)* Edouard? I know, I know. My mother refuses
further treatment. Why don't you speak to her? Try. Thanks.
*(Hangs up the phone. Raises his hand to his forehead. Presses his
head with his fingers)* She had a mastectomy and went through
chemotherapy … She doesn't want any more. "It's not living that
matters, it's living well." Mother says that, and I agree, but … It
does no good to know that for her life is no longer worth living
and has become synonymous with borrowed time. Knowing
is one thing, accepting is another. I wonder if my sister's at
home. *(He picks up the phone and dials. A pause. He hangs up)*
Answering machine.

SCENE 6

(Seriema and the Doctor are seated face to face. Silence)

DOCTOR
(Soliloquy) Did Seriema come here to say nothing? If she at least
talked, I could stop thinking about death, about the passage of
time. *(To Seriema)* Here you can speak freely. Nothing you say
will be censured.

SERIEMA
It never occurred to me that you could censure me. Otherwise I
wouldn't come. I thought it strange that you called asking what
time I would be at your office ... I never heard of an analyst
doing that. You must have guessed I didn't want to come.

DOCTOR
But you came. Talk.

SERIEMA
(Irritated) I don't have any way of saying what I want. Because,
in your language, I don't know the word ...

DOCTOR
What word?

SERIEMA
Saudade. Without that word, I'm not who I am. I miss the
language of Brazil. *Bonjour* and I miss my country, *bom dia.*
Bonsoir is strange, because *bonsoir* doesn't exist in my language,
only good night, *boa noite, bonne nuit.* Because night falls there
in the blink of an eye. Here, when I say a word wrong, the person
I'm talking to first corrects me and only afterward listens to what
I mean to say. And it's impossible not to make mistakes. In French
sea is *la mer*, feminine; in Portuguese, it's *o mar*, masculine. *Banco*,
bank, in French is feminine, *la banque.* But no matter how often I
go to the bank, I always say *le banque*—I get it wrong.

DOCTOR
(Soliloquy) Is she going to go on with that list? There's not a
session when she doesn't talk about the language problem. That
allows her to skirt what's really important, the essential.

SERIEMA
But the worst is what happened to our samba. *O samba*,
masculine, became *la samba* ... Everything is turned around.

Tree, palm, fruit—in French they're masculine, not feminine.
Even the sex of a ball is different.

DOCTOR
The masculine sex of words, the feminine sex, sex … *(Seriema
abruptly turns away from the Doctor's gaze. She stares at the
couch. Then she gets up and throws herself onto it. Following her
movement, the Doctor sits down in the armchair)* You didn't go to
the couch, you conquered it! From now on, it's yours.

SERIEMA
(Pause. Ironically) The couch is mine … To say what? That I
sleep alone every night? I don't even remember anymore what
sex is like. Or rather, I do. But sex without love doesn't count.
With him, at least—

DOCTOR
With whom?

SERIEMA
Antonio. With him I at least had the illusion of love. I thought
he loved me … My happiness was clear as day.

DOCTOR
And now you think you were mistaken? That he didn't love you?

SERIEMA
(Pause) I don't know what I think anymore.

DOCTOR
(Seriema raises her head and stares at the Doctor) And? Speak.

SERIEMA
I remembered something my father told me shortly before he
died: "Don't forget that I love you." It seemed like a demand.

DOCTOR
It was. *(Emphatically)* And you haven't forgotten him … *(The Doctor
stands up. Seriema pays and leaves)* Well, the face-to-face is over.
Seriema no longer needs to look at me. She can lie down and listen
to herself. It was a victory. People live their lives without listening
to themselves, with a tin ear. Some even die without ever having
listened to themselves, eternally deaf to themselves … to their own
body, which screams rather than talks. A deafness that in itself is
enough to justify psychoanalysis. If it even still needs to be justified.

(From this session to the end, Seriema will go to the couch)

ACT II

SCENE 1

(The armchairs are in the dark and the light is focused on the couch. The window, barely visible at the start of the act, becomes more noticeable as the play advances. Seriema enters, frightened, and lies down)

DOCTOR
What happened? Talk.

SERIEMA
(Pause. Abruptly) What happened was that I had a hallucination. That never happened to me before.

DOCTOR
A hallucination ... *(Without changing his tone)* And what was it?

SERIEMA
What was it? I saw—

DOCTOR
Speak.

SERIEMA
(Softly) Rats. *(Disgusted)* I saw rats in the waiting room. The other patient said there weren't any, but I saw them ... I saw two.

DOCTOR
Two what?

SERIEMA
Two huge, black, horrible rats.

DOCTOR
(Puzzled) Two rats?

SERIEMA
(Pause) That's strange!

DOCTOR
What?

SERIEMA
When you pronounced the word, I suddenly realized that *ra* is the first syllable of my father's name ... and my great-grandfather's.

DOCTOR
What is the name?

SERIEMA
Raji ... My great-grandfather was called Raji. And it was to
keep himself from being executed that he emigrated ... so his
children could revere their saints, live in peace, and bury their
dead. He died on the ship and, to avoid the plague, was thrown
into the sea. The body was wrapped in a shroud. Bible verses ...
farewell ... *alla cum mag.*

DOCTOR
Hmm.

SERIEMA
He left Lebanon, but he never arrived in Brazil.

DOCTOR
He did arrive. Otherwise you wouldn't be talking about him.

SERIEMA
Till today I had never spoken of him. Just as I never said the
name of my father when I was a child. "What's your father's
name?" "Roberto ... Ricardo ..." I never said Raji. Why should I
run the risk of being called a Turk? *(Seriema covers her face with
her hands)*

DOCTOR
(Affectionately) What matters, my dear, is that now you can say
the name. That you can tell the truth. There is no way to forever
deny one's origins ... renounce one's ancestors. Life depends on
what we can say ... Your life has changed.

SERIEMA
What about the hallucination?

DOCTOR
You won't have it again.

SERIEMA
What? I don't—

DOCTOR
The name you silenced to hide your origins has materialized
... Materialized in the rat. Now you can say Raji. There's no
more cause for hallucination. You're no longer subject to an
unexpected apparition of your father ... *(The Doctor stands up)*
Come back tomorrow. *(Seriema gets up, pays, and leaves)* It's

horrible not being able to be Arab, Jew, black ... Not being able to
be who you are ... Nothing is worse than racism turned inward.
Seriema is cured of that ... She was cured today, here in analysis.
(Pause) I'm the one who needs analysis now, because I can't
accept my mother's decision. She's categorical: "Only palliative
care." She was always opposed to the therapeutic fury, but death
means *never again* ... Never again "Good morning, son."

SCENE 2

(The Doctor in the chair and Seriema on the couch)

SERIEMA
I dreamed about my father. He died so long ago!

DOCTOR
The dream, what was it like?

SERIEMA
I was at a judo center, near the house where I lived as a child. I
was the only girl in the center. Wearing white and ready to spar
... and a yellow belt on my waist.

DOCTOR
Yellow?

SERIEMA
Yes, for beginners. My father was sitting down and showing
me the black belt of champions. He wanted to watch the fight.
Suddenly, the instructor bursts into the room and demands he
return the black belt. I scream and run out. My father catches
up to me in the street, takes me by the arm, and pulls from his
pocket another black belt, laughing loudly.

DOCTOR
An unbeatable father!

SERIEMA
He wanted me to be unbeatable, a champion at judo, karate,
whatever ... Everything the boys in the neighborhood did, I did.
My father would say, "You were born to be like them. If boys can
learn, so can you!" Anything my father wanted, I wanted ... Sports
and studies. I was brought up to compete, to win contests, grants ...

DOCTOR
That's why you're here ... You came on a grant, didn't you?

SERIEMA
(Pause. Ironically) I won the grant after losing my life, the child
I conceived. I miscarried instead of giving birth. It would have
been better to be born sterile and not have built up expectations.

DOCTOR
What is the relationship between having lost the child and your
story?

SERIEMA
What story?

DOCTOR
Your childhood ... your father.

SERIEMA
My father is dead and buried!

DOCTOR
Buried doesn't mean forgotten. Your dream is proof of that.

SERIEMA
He died after raising me to love only him. "Don't forget that you can always count on me. No one is ever going to love you the way I do." Always, never ...

DOCTOR
What else?

SERIEMA
He would pick me up at school and want to know if some boy had spoken to me. When I told him no, and repeated *the same thing* every day, he would smile. Then he'd ask, "What would you have done?" I said I would have hit the boy. And he said, "Good for you." He couldn't accept that I would be interested in anyone else. He wanted me only for himself. *(Seriema covers her face with her hands)*

DOCTOR
(Soliloquy) He definitely did everything he could to turn his daughter against men ... half of humanity. No wonder she's in analysis. *(To Seriema)* What's important is that you have remembered the story.

SERIEMA
Important why?

DOCTOR
Because whoever ignores the past becomes its victim, goes on repeating, and can't reinvent his life. *(He stands up. Seriema pays and leaves)* She didn't want to know about her father, but he returned in her dream. Ancestors return, they don't cease to exist. That's my consolation. When Mother is no more, she'll still be with me in dreams and in memory ... to tell me it's necessary to live well.

SCENE 3

(The Doctor in the chair and Seriema on the couch)

SERIEMA
I left here in bad shape. I'm paying just to suffer. I don't know if I
should continue.
(Silence)

DOCTOR
Why did you leave in bad shape?

SERIEMA
I left feeling ashamed of my father ... and I remembered other
embarrassing things.

DOCTOR
You can talk here. You must ... I'm here to listen.

SERIEMA
(Pause) My breasts ... When they began to grow, I was ashamed!
And the nipple that became hard as a rock. It hurt and meant a
body of a woman. Suddenly, I was no longer sexless.

DOCTOR
You were no longer sexless?

SERIEMA
Yes. I was no longer sexless. Before that rock-hard nipple,
sex didn't exist. From then on, it was one embarrassment
after another. The pubic hair, the blood every month ...
menstruation. I would writhe in pain from cramps and felt
disgust. Whether I wanted it or not, I was no longer like my
father. And, like my mother, I didn't want to be ... She lived for
the church. To her, everything was a sin. The word *freedom* was
meaningless. Luckily, it was Maria who raised me.

DOCTOR
You were as ashamed of your body as of your origins ... Your
body contradicted your desire to remain sexless.

SERIEMA
(Ironically) "If boys can learn, so can you!" And I imagined I
was like them. *(Laughs)* Nonsense! I only had the right to do
what my father wanted. And when I met my first boyfriend, he
stopped talking to me. He wanted to kill me.

DOCTOR
Really?

SERIEMA
If it weren't for Maria …
(Semidarkness. The sound of bossa nova. Maria's voice offstage, then she enters dancing)

MARIA'S VOICE OFFSTAGE
Why do you mistreat yourself? There's nothing wrong with you, Seriema. Your father is jealous. The jealous heart is jealous because it is. Pay no attention … What matters is how you feel … Pay it no mind, let it be. Come, my love … Vem coração. Me dá a mão. Não liga não. Vem, vem, vem coração
(Maria exits. Office lighting returns)

SERIEMA
Maria gave me strength. But my father was devastated and I no longer found pleasure in the courtship. I wanted to dump my boyfriend and in the end he dumped me.

DOCTOR
(Soliloquy) One more victim of jealousy … of the tyranny of jealousy.

SERIEMA
I didn't know pleasure when I met Antonio. He inflamed me. I liked what I felt … Sex was never the same again, and I went far. I put away shame. For us, the word *sin* had no meaning. With him, I didn't know who was man and who was woman; each of us could be one or the other. If it hadn't been for the miscarriage—Antonio told me I didn't want his child. *(Pause)* That was at the hospital, just after the hemorrhage and the operation on my uterus. From that moment on, nothing went right. I was cured but had no husband.

DOCTOR
(Emphatically) And you did want to have Antonio's child?

SERIEMA
(Pause) I don't know. *(The Doctor rises)* I say *I don't know* and you get up.

DOCTOR
True.

SERIEMA
You're going to leave me with *I don't know*? I can't stand this way
of ending a session … this sudden brutal interruption. *(Seriema
rises and is about to leave without paying)*

DOCTOR
Fifty euros.

SERIEMA
I didn't withdraw any money.

DOCTOR
Then go and get it.

SERIEMA
(Soliloquy at the office door) I'll come back tomorrow. Today I'm
taking a break from the unconscious!

SCENE 4

(The Doctor waits for Seriema sitting in his armchair)

DOCTOR
(Soliloquy) A being without sex is what Seriema wanted to be.
Because biological sex ran counter to her fantasy ... the fantasy
of being like her father.

SERIEMA
(She enters agitated and immediately lies down) I'm late because
Antonio called. It was last night. He said he needed to see me.
I simply told him that I'm in Paris. He hung up and called back.
"You're there ... then that's where I'm going." I was puzzled.

DOCTOR
Not without reason.

SERIEMA
And now I'm confused.

DOCTOR
Hmm.
(Silence)

SERIEMA
This business of paying every time I come here bothers me. I
don't understand why it has to be that way. It'd be better if it
wasn't.

DOCTOR
For you to forget that you pay me ... that I'm your analyst.
Unconditional love is what you want.

SERIEMA
I don't deny it. I wanted to be loved unconditionally by Antonio,
with or without a child. I wanted to be loved just as I loved. I got
pregnant twice because that's what he wanted.

DOCTOR
(Soliloquy) She got pregnant to satisfy her husband! Truly an
aberration ... That's what it means to be the object of desire
of the other ... *(To Seriema)* You only wanted what Antonio
wanted ... just like in your childhood.

SERIEMA
I don't understand.

DOCTOR
In childhood, you only wanted what your father wanted ... You
didn't speak with anyone at school ... with any boy.

SERIEMA
(Pause) True. And later ... without being aware of it, I lived only
to satisfy Antonio.

DOCTOR
Except that you got pregnant and didn't give birth. The desire to
satisfy your husband wasn't realized ... Why?

SERIEMA
You only listen to what I say in order to find out something else.

DOCTOR
(Soliloquy) She's evading again. If she could, she'd argue
analytical theory with me just to continue in ignorance ... to not
do the analysis.

SERIEMA
You ask questions ... Answers, you never give me. And today I
have nothing to say. I can't take any more. May I leave? I want to
sleep. Last night, after the phone call, I didn't sleep a wink. I kept
thinking about what I should do.

DOCTOR
See you next week. *(He stands up)*

SERIEMA
Next week?

DOCTOR
The holiday ... because of the holiday.

SERIEMA
(Gets up. Ironically) Have a nice holiday. *(She pays and leaves)*

DOCTOR
(Standing, walking) She's prettier when she's irritated. As much
feminine as masculine. There's nothing sexless about her. That's
why she loves Antonio ... "With him, I didn't know who was
man and who was woman; each of us could be one or the other."

Seriema doesn't insist on being one or the other, she has a freedom
that I lack … I've never had an experience like hers. Or rather, I
may have had one but would never dare to say it. Say I didn't know
if I was man or woman? Never. Fear of being homosexual—as
if that were a perversion—as if bisexuality didn't exist. I studied
but didn't learn what I studied … It's not enough to study theory
in order to recognize one's own bisexuality … Seriema's freedom
astounds me.

SCENE 5

(The Doctor in his chair and Seriema sitting up on the couch)

DOCTOR
Better to lie down. *(Seriema puts one leg on the couch)*

SERIEMA
I wasn't even going to come today.

DOCTOR
But you came, and that's what matters. And you're here on the couch, lying down … *(Seriema doesn't change positions, and the Doctor doesn't insist. Soliloquy)* I can't insist on the correct position. I can't take the chance that she'll leave and interrupt her analysis … I have to be cool.

SERIEMA
(Pause) Friday I forgot the key to my apartment and couldn't get into the building. I had to wait in the street until my neighbor showed up, till three in the morning. I got sick and spent all weekend in bed. *(Emphatically)* And, yesterday, what I had wasn't a dream, it was a nightmare!

DOCTOR
I'm listening.

SERIEMA
(Ironically) "I'm listening." If I hadn't spoken about my father, I wouldn't have had the nightmare. I woke up so frightened that I cut myself … I hit my head on the glass door in the bathroom. I can't take this analysis anymore.

DOCTOR
But what was it you dreamed?

SERIEMA
I can't tell you.

DOCTOR
You can. Here, you can.

SERIEMA
(Lies down) A bubble. I was in a red bubble … sleeping on the floor. Suddenly, I heard a whistle and a voice saying, "Time to wake up now." It was what my father would say every morning.

DOCTOR
And what else?

SERIEMA
(Pause) I wake up and see the floor of the floating bubble. I stretch and get up carefully so I don't fall. I walk as if I were on a tightrope. At every step, the voice: *"Mens sana in corpore sano."* Another favorite saying of my father's. I stop and look at the red, which lightens in color and changes into a glaring brilliance ... Suddenly, he appears.

DOCTOR
Who appears?

SERIEMA
My father ... *(She falls silent and covers her face with her hands)*

DOCTOR
What are you ashamed of?

SERIEMA
Of what happened.

DOCTOR
(Softly) Tell me.

SERIEMA
(Agitated) My father hands me a newborn that he's holding in his arms. "Take him, take our son." *(Beside herself)* "Our son ..." That's incest! *(Seriema crosses her arms over her chest and turns her head away to hide her face)* The child of insanity, of my father's morbid jealousy and my own submission. *(Bitterly)* *Mens sana in corpore sano.* I woke up as if I'd just left hell. Incest is a crime ... an abjection. I'm afraid ... I'm afraid I'm going crazy!

DOCTOR
Stay calm. The fantasy of incest isn't incest, and no one goes crazy by wanting to be.

SERIEMA
Hmm.

DOCTOR
It's true that an incest fantasy isn't innocuous.

SERIEMA
I don't understand what you mean.

DOCTOR
If not for the incest fantasy, you wouldn't be here today, you
wouldn't have sought treatment … You could have had Antonio's
child. But the father of your child, to you, wasn't Antonio.

SERIEMA
Now I understand even less.

DOCTOR
The father of your child, in your fantasy, was not Antonio … but
your father. *(Pause)* The unconscious exists, we are all subject
to it. *(The Doctor stands up)* Come. You're no longer unaware
of what you needed to know. *(Seriema remains seated)* Come,
Seriema. *(She rises mechanically, pays, and leaves)* "My desire
will be yours." A father who shackled his daughter … kept her
from even imagining a father for her own child … and thus
made motherhood impossible. The unconscious exists and it
isn't the little lamb of a good shepherd. But Seriema has taken a
giant step and broken the shackles. She's no longer the slave of
repetition.

SCENE 6

(The Doctor in sitting his chair, alone)

DOCTOR
Half an hour late. One step forward, one step back.

SERIEMA
(Seriema comes in and doesn't lie down but remains standing) I'm
in no condition to do the session and I don't even know if I'm
going to stay in France.

DOCTOR
Why?

SERIEMA
I lost the eye.

DOCTOR
What?

SERIEMA
Coming out of the telephone booth.

DOCTOR
Did you hurt yourself again? You lost an eye?

SERIEMA
The glass eye, the pendant. My protector.

DOCTOR
How did it happen?

SERIEMA
Uh … in the booth.

DOCTOR
Where?

SERIEMA
(Hesitantly) In the booth where I disconnect the telephone.

DOCTOR
(Without censure) You disconnect the telephone?

SERIEMA
Yes … to talk to Brazil. All Brazilians do it.

DOCTOR
And how was it that you lost the fetish, the protector?

SERIEMA
I don't know. I only know that nothing else matters to me.

DOCTOR
(Imperatively) Go back to the booth, look for the eye. If you don't find it, call Brazil, order another one right away. *(Seriema leaves)* Without the pendant, Seriema won't stay, and I'm here so she'll stay. Look for it, make a phone call, send a telegram … Anything for her to continue analysis till the end. If it's necessary for me to act like a guru, I'll become a guru. The analyst is an actor who pretends not to be acting, he can take on any role. Just because I'm French doesn't mean I'm not Brazilian. Even without believing in magic.

SCENE 7

(The Doctor in his chair and Seriema on the couch, in feminine clothing)

SERIEMA
In the waiting room I saw rats … Today, I dozed off and dreamed you were dead and in a coffin. From time to time you would get up and console the people present, say *adieu*. As if you were a fantasy.

DOCTOR
How so, a fantasy?

SERIEMA
No, I made a mistake. I meant to say *phantom*—as if you were a *phantom*—but I misspoke. *(Pause)* In French, I get confused. Two languages so similar and yet so different! I even think you were dead because—

DOCTOR
Because of what?

SERIEMA
(Pause) If you died, I would go back to Brazil … here I stumble over words, stumble and fall, words seem like stones in the road. They're only good for me to communicate. "What does it cost?" "Give me change." "Please pass the bread." They don't take me back to anything, they're opaque, they're like things.

DOCTOR
(Tenderly) What about the other words, the ones in Portuguese?

SERIEMA
I was born and brought up with them … they have more than one meaning, they take me back to other times, other places … I don't make use of words just to achieve this or that. With them I play and find joy, I invent, I surprise myself. My language is my joy. And I need the relief it gives me. In Portuguese, I feel safe. I have the certainty of being able to say what I mean. *(Pause)* Besides, I've had enough of living without sunshine. The French say that the sun shines for everyone, but here I never see the sun. What did I do wrong to be so far from home? Antonio calls me every day, asking me to return. He's the man I love … and want to have a child with.

DOCTOR
(Emphatically) The man you want to have a child with … Then you've chosen the father! Antonio!

SERIEMA
(Pause) I've chosen.

DOCTOR
(Soliloquy) Now she'll leave …

SERIEMA
I want his child … a child born there, who speaks my language.

DOCTOR
Hmm. And what else?

SERIEMA
(Laughs) You're not interested in what I say but in what's left unsaid.

DOCTOR
That's true. See you tomorrow. *(Seriema pays and leaves)* What interests an analyst if not the part that's left unsaid? The fact is that a child is now within Seriema's reach … Now she can give life because she can choose the father. She has stopped being against herself. Analysis is over. *(Pause)* No, analysis will only be over when Seriema understands why she chose an analyst whose language isn't her own, since for her, language is fundamental.

SCENE 8

(The Doctor in his chair. Seriema enters and sits on the couch)

SERIEMA
(Pause) It's not easy to say …

DOCTOR
Hmm.

SERIEMA
The time has come to go home … I don't want to stay here forever. And I don't have anything more to say.

DOCTOR
I think you do. Maybe now you can tell me why you did an analysis in a language that's not yours.

SERIEMA
I don't know. *(Pause)* Maybe it was—

DOCTOR
Yes, yes?

SERIEMA
(Hesitating) Maybe it was in order to not say everything.

DOCTOR
How so?

SERIEMA
My father always said he was the only one I could tell everything.

DOCTOR
(Soliloquy) My God!

SERIEMA
(Pause) It was to do what my father wanted that I chose you … in order to not say everything. I chose an analyst who didn't know my language. So as not to reveal myself … Unbelievable! An aberration!

DOCTOR
No, my dear. It was an unconscious act.

SERIEMA
Choosing an analyst to obey my father?

DOCTOR
The unconscious acts and speaks for us. And no one can be held responsible for what he does without being conscious of it.

SERIEMA
What madness!

DOCTOR
A madness that was the condition of your analysis. I had to accept your choice so that you could move ahead. *(Pause)* Now you're free … free of your father's desire.

SERIEMA
Free of my father's desire?

DOCTOR
Yes. Now you can follow your own path.

SERIEMA
(In a low voice) Is it over?

DOCTOR
Like it or not. Of course. You didn't gain your freedom from your father just to be tied to the analyst.

SERIEMA
(With confidence) The analysis is over. Brazil … Antonio is waiting for me.

DOCTOR
Seriema …

SERIEMA
Adieu.

DOCTOR
Adeus.

SERIEMA
Goodbye, Doctor.

(The characters remain motionless. The distant sound of samba. Semidarkness. Maria enters, dancing)

THE END

AN INTERVIEW WITH MARI RUTI

Translated by Chris Vanderwees

Mari Ruti: *I am very grateful that you have agreed to this interview.
I must say that I find your memoir spectacular. A first-hand account
of being analyzed by Lacan is not something that one comes across
every day. And you do a fabulous job of conveying the intimacy of the
experience to the reader, who feels like she is right there with you in
Lacan's consulting room. Michèle Sarde is right when she says that you
shed light on the mysterious nature of Lacan's clinical practice. Many
of us are intrigued by this practice, especially the short session, which
means that you have given us a rare gift by granting us a glimpse into
what went on at 5, rue de Lille.*

*Let me start from where your story begins. In 1971, you went to Paris
to ask Lacan if he knew an analyst who could teach Lacanian theory in
Brazil. At that point you were a psychiatrist. But you were also already
immersed in psychoanalysis, especially Lacanian theory. How did this
come about?*

Betty Milan: My father was a doctor, and he wanted me to follow
in his footsteps. I entered the Faculty of Medicine in São Paulo in
1962 when I was eighteen years old. It was quite an achievement. The
competition was very difficult and few women were admitted. In my
class, there were five women and ninety-five men. My success cost me
dearly. The young man I had been dating since I was fourteen left me.
Was he envious or jealous? The fact is that after this abandonment
I was bruised and terribly anguished. I started an analysis with a
"Kleinian" from São Paulo—a training analyst from the Brazilian
Psychoanalytic Society (BPS).

Returning to my background, I started working in psychiatry in
1964, and then I discovered analytic theory, which I immersed myself
in immediately. In 1966, my analyst urged me to apply for training
at the BPS, where I was accepted. But two years later I stopped my
analysis. I considered it finished. The BPS disagreed and told me that
if I did not resume the analysis, I could not continue my training. I did
not want to continue. Shortly afterward, I met a French psychoanalyst
who was passing through São Paulo and who worked with Lacan.
Lacan's discourse interested me greatly, and so I formed, with other
doctors and psychologists, a group to read the *Écrits*. A French-
speaking professor helped us decipher the texts.

My first contact with Lacan was therefore through his texts. In
1971, three years later, I met him in Paris.

MR: *Can you please clarify the trajectory of your career? When you
first met Lacan in 1971, you were already a practicing psychiatrist in*

Brazil. You said in your memoir that you wanted to be recognized as a psychoanalyst abroad so that you could then practice in Brazil? Why is this?

BM: At that time, I was a doctor and I had my diploma in psychiatry. I could practice psychiatry, but with psychoanalysis, things were more complicated. I had been studying psychoanalytic theory since 1964 and undergone a four-year analysis. The BPS course was not compulsory, but all Brazilian analysts took it. It was the door that opened [*Sésame*] onto the analytical community—all Brazilian analysts had followed this route—but I was excluded because I did not want to continue my analysis. Therefore, I needed an external and irrefutable recognition, which I went to seek in Paris from Lacan. French education was highly valued in Brazil, and the Doctor's guarantee was worth all the courses in the world. An analysis with Lacan assured me the recognition I needed.

MR: *During your 1971 visit to Paris, you met with Lacan three times. My understanding is that prior to these meetings, you had no plans to enter into analysis with him. What was it about the meetings that gave rise to that desire?*

BM: The group that was reading the *Écrits* wanted to invite a French Lacanian analyst to work with us and give conferences in São Paulo. So I went to Lacan on a professional level to ask him to appoint an analyst for the work. I had no intention of doing an analysis with him. It was Lacan who saw me as his future analysand. He made sure that I finally expressed my wish—which had remained latent until then—to return to Paris to do an analysis with him after I had finished the work that I had started in Brazil with a very brilliant psychiatrist. The Doctor let me know that he would wait, and I left for Brazil with a commitment to return to France two years later.

MR: *When you started your analysis, your French was not yet fluent. Because of this, Lacan suggested that you might want to consult a Portuguese analyst instead of him. Your memoir makes it clear why you did not want a Portuguese analyst. For instance, you mention the considerable difference between Brazilian Portuguese and the Portuguese spoken in Portugal. And you were extremely insistent that the analysis had to be with Lacan or not at all. Why is this?*

BM: The reasons I had to stop my training at the Brazilian Psychoanalytic Society were never very clear. Lacan himself had been excluded from the International Psychoanalytic Society in the early 1960s because of the short session. It was an injustice, and I identified with him. But that is not enough to explain my insistence … What motivated me was perhaps the knowledge I already had of his theoretical work, and also our initial talks, his way of being, his benevolence, his assurance, and his humor. Laughter is highly valued in Brazilian culture. It is not by chance that I write satires. That said, transference operates like love, in which there is always something enigmatic. Fernando Pessoa expresses the matter with the question he asks about love: "Angel, what substance are your wings made of?" It is undeniable that I formed a transference to the Doctor very quickly.

MR: *Speaking of transference, you repeatedly suggest that Lacan kept the analysis going, that he encouraged you to keep coming to the sessions. How did he manage this?*

BM: He always left me with a riddle, which I had to decipher. Once I had done so, I wanted to talk to him about it and I would return to his consulting room.

MR: *Your memoir places a great deal of emphasis on Lacan's practice of the short session. Presumably you were familiar with the concept from having read Lacanian theory before the beginning of your analysis with Lacan in 1973. Still, were you startled the first time he cut a session short? What did it feel like when he stood up and delivered his* See you tomorrow, dear? *Did it feel appropriate? Or did it feel upsetting or unsettling? Did it take you some time to get used to your sessions being interrupted unexpectedly?*

BM: Yes, I was confused the first time he cut the session short, which was right at the beginning. I had agreed with him in 1971 that I would return in two years, and when I phoned him in 1973 to say that I had arrived, he simply said, "So what?" That's how he elicited the answer that threw me into analysis: "So I want to do an analysis!" I must say that his abruptness felt violent. Then he told me to come back the next day and hung up. This was particularly effective. He had made me express my desire clearly. After that, I got used to the cut because it made me listen to myself, to reflect upon myself, and I realized that I liked it. Inner speech is very important for a writer, and it is in France that the possibility of writing opened up for me—but I did not know yet that I was going to write.

MR: *Were there times when you wished that he had not cut the session when he did?*

BM: It was rather his silences that intrigued me. I don't remember being upset by a cut. Each time he interrupted the session, Lacan offered me the possibility of deciphering an enigma, and that is what encouraged me to continue. I probably played the game spontaneously and adopted the process without questioning its merits. Perhaps because it was "going somewhere" [ça marchait], quite simply. The cut was part of my path, but certainly not of everyone who did an analysis with Lacan: he did not proceed in the same way with everyone. What mattered to him was to make analysis possible. Above all, "avoid the rupture" [Primo non rompere] was his motto.

MR: *It is obvious from your account that the short session worked extremely well for you. You were able to leave Lacan's consulting room and to mull over the reasons for why he chose a specific moment in the session to cut it. In addition, you seemed to frequently arrive at important insights about the personal dilemmas you were dealing with precisely because he had interrupted the session at a moment when something essential or important had arisen. Why do you think that the short session worked so well for you?*

BM: I quickly took the bait. I liked to reflect on my speech and to decode the reason for the cut. Each time, it was a bit like a challenge to myself. But do not believe that I happened to discover something essential about myself at each session. There were many sessions where nothing happened, as is the case in any analysis, where all the sessions do not have the same weight. In my memoir, I retained what truly mattered, and this was possible because previously I had written a novel and a play. We may consider these as a kind of training to arrive at something very simple: it was the passage through fiction that allowed me to write a memoir where what was important was Lacan's way of working and no longer my personal story. *Why Lacan* has nothing to do with an ego trip.

MR: *Let me restate the question slightly differently. Do you think that there was something about you as an analysand—or even about your personality—that made you an ideal candidate for the successful use of the short session? In other words, do you think that another kind of analysand might not have responded as dexterously and creatively to the challenge of doing so much of the analytic work herself? I suppose I am asking whether you believe that the short session is appropriate for all analysands or whether it takes a certain kind of person to be able to tolerate its abruptness?*

BM: It is not a question of short or long sessions. It is up to the analyst to find the right way to work with the analysand that he has in front of him. The timing of my sessions is always variable, as was Lacan's. The short session has the advantage of precipitating the manifestation of the unconscious, but it is not a universal panacea. Analysis does not exist to respond to the demand for unconditional love, but to ensure that the analysand remembers their history so as not to repeat it, so that they manage to reinvent themselves. This point is very clear. That said, not everyone is made for analysis. But an analysis that reinforces the ego is contrary to the path opened by Freud. This is not what Lacan did when he worked with me. He did not reinforce my ego even when I was depressed. To know how he handled this, you have to read my memoir.

MR: *In Anglo-American circles, Lacan often has the reputation of having been a cold, even callous analyst. There are elements of your account that point in this direction. But I have to say that what most surprised me about the dynamic between the two of you was the warmth and compassion that he seemed to show whenever you needed it. I was also quite startled by the repetition of the word* dear *in Lacan's speech as well as by the intensity of his attention that comes across in the* Tell me *and* I'm listening *that he repeatedly used to prompt you to keep speaking. You note that your transference to Lacan was intense. How did you experience him as an analyst? What was the "temperature" (the atmosphere) of the analytic sessions like? Did it lean toward cold indifference, as some Anglo-American readers might expect? Or did it lean toward warmth and compassion? Or did the tenor change from session to session, depending on the content of the issues discussed?*

BM: Lacan was confident without resorting to familiarity; he was flexible without being unctuous. He exuded a form of natural authority and of great mental power, but without ever giving the impression of dominating or invading; rather, he accompanied you. You always felt that he was very close to you, his patient, especially at difficult moments, when you were close to a block or a break. And when he interrupted the session, he could be terse without ever being cold. In a word, he had a lot of humanity.

On the other hand, your question reminds me of soccer coaches on the sidelines, who are constantly challenging their players during the game. Lacan also made you go forward. He was never there to waste his time or yours. He did not think that *time is money* but rather that *time is life*. Nothing to do with indifference. It is not by chance that he introduced into his theory the desire of the analyst and also the resistance of the analyst. Lacan did not resist analysis in the same way that a writer does not resist writing. A writer obliges herself to have discipline and endures patiently, not knowing where she is going. Hence the kinship between the psychoanalyst and the artist. Psychoanalytic theory is a matter of scientific observation, but its practice is an art.

MR: *Your analysis was obviously very successful. What were the components of Lacan's clinical practice that you found especially generative? And were there things that bothered you, that you wish had gone differently? Were there moments of negative transference that could have been prevented by a different approach? Or is negative transference an inevitable component of analysis?*

BM: I don't think that negative transference is inevitable. But it is difficult to avoid, and I believe it is attributable to the analyst. During my analysis, Lacan once responded to a provocation from me. I told him that he classified his analysands according to their neuroses, and he replied affirmatively, knowing that this would upset me, although this was not the issue at stake. This aroused a negative transference in me. He must have been annoyed that day—and I probably was too. We know that perfection is not of this world …

MR: *The moment when you transitioned from face-to-face analysis to the couch was initiated by you rather than by Lacan. You quite simply walked to the couch and lay down. Do you remember what caused you to want to do so? How did it change the analytic dynamic for you? Do you think that there are things in analysis that can only happen on the couch—that require the couch?*

BM: This is an interesting question. I was the one who took the initiative to seize the couch, and this shows to what extent Lacan allowed the analysand to do their analysis. I did not think about this at the time. I don't remember what made me go from face-to-face to the couch. But I know that I immediately started to cry and that Lacan consoled me with a sentence that I have not forgotten: "There is no reason to despair. You have masterfully taken possession of this couch! Now, it is yours." It was as if I had just arrived at the top of a mountain without finding my breath and someone had reached out to me. On the couch, I was freer to associate and deepen my analysis. I'm not sure that the use of the couch should be systematic. Since the pandemic, I have been working a lot with WhatsApp, without image, just with voice. What I am sure of is that it takes time to move into free association.

MR: *You make it clear that the goal of Lacanian analysis is to promote the analysand's independence rather than dependence, that Lacan wanted his analysands to realize that he did not possess the answers to their psychic impasses but that it was up to them to arrive at the answers themselves. He wanted to dissolve the illusion that he was the subject-supposed-to-know. I get the impression that you very much appreciated this aspect of his clinical practice. You seemed to become self-reliant quickly and without much difficulty. Is this how you experienced the matter? Or did it take some effort to shift the responsibility for analytic work from Lacan to yourself?*

BM: I appreciate your reading of my memoir: it is very precise. But the readiness with which I was able to accept the cut is also due to the fact that I had done several years of analysis in Brazil and that I was already an analyst. To put it another way, I appreciated the way Lacan did things because I perceived his approach, so to speak, internally: I myself had practiced as an analyst. Still, I made many discoveries with a practitioner such as the Doctor.

MR: *It makes a great deal of sense that, as an analyst yourself, you were able to appreciate Lacan's distinctive methodology. Still, a moment that stands out in your narrative that I imagine might have wounded even an experienced analysand is when you showed Lacan your Portuguese translation of his seminar on* Freud's Papers on Technique, *and he failed to acknowledge the immense amount of labor that you had put into the project. I know that this was toward the end of the analysis, but it nevertheless sounds like a potentially damaging response. How were you able to overcome negative transference at that moment and to continue the analysis?*

BM: It's true, I was surprised and upset. Lacan had supported me throughout this work—and it was a very significant work, for it was necessary to keep the tone of the lectures and the rather particular formulas of the Doctor—but as soon as it was completed, he just told me that it was not his language. His answer made me decide later not to live and work in a language that was not my own. But he also made me realize how concerned I was with translation as a process. I was destined by the emigration of my ancestors to live between languages, as one swims between two waters, and I must say that translation has brought a lot to the writer that I am: it made me discover the language in which I write my fiction, the Portuguese language. Maybe one day I will write in another language. But I'm not certain. It feels so good to write with confidence …

MR: *There were several core dilemmas that you worked through during your analysis. The first to emerge seemed to be the question of origins, your predicament of being the descendant of Lebanese immigrants to Brazil and the xenophobia—many Anglo-American readers might use the word racism—that you experienced in Brazil due to your ethnicity and skin color. Would you say that your analysis with Lacan helped you to process the wounding experiences that you had had?*

BM: My ancestors were victims of xenophobia from native Brazilians and so was I, the third generation. It is strange that I never talked about it in the analysis I did in Brazil with a Jewish analyst. It was completely repressed. It was because I met Lacan and did my analysis in French that I was able to overcome this repression. And it is now that I realize it. This is an important discovery. It shows that doing an analysis in a language that is not one's mother tongue can allow one to go far beyond. Dominique Marin, a French psychoanalyst who works on the links between psychoanalysis and literature, author of *Lacan and Beckett*, asked me in an interview I gave him for the *l'En je* journal if I had gone into exile in a language that was not my own in order to better undergo my analysis. This is exactly right. I went into exile in France and in the French language. We know how important exile is for a writer, but I think that it can also be crucial for an analysand. I had never discussed the subject of immigration with my Brazilian analyst and I spoke about it with Lacan as soon as I met him. The passage from one culture to another necessarily has effects on one's discourse.

MR: *Related to your response is the fact that, in addition to not speaking your native tongue, Lacan did not know much about Brazil. As much as you loved Paris, you were homesick a lot. And you especially missed the comfort of Portuguese as a language that made you feel at home. Yet you just suggested that the points of "disconnection" between you and Lacan—the lacunae in his knowledge and his inability to speak your language—ended up being productive for your analysis rather than impeding it. Did I interpret this correctly?*

BM: Yes, yes, your interpretation is correct. The fact that he did not know Portuguese was very productive, and I realized through my novel *Le Perroquet de Lacan* that I also chose the Doctor as my analyst because of this ignorance. It allowed me to remain veiled in front of the analyst as my father wished me to always be. In other words, it replicated the dynamic that I had with my father, who was very jealous and who wanted me to perform in a certain way to the outside world. Seriema, the protagonist of the play, *Goodbye Doctor*, evokes the jealousy of her father. My father, who died of leukemia at the age of forty-eight, played a major role in my life. I largely owe him my education and the authorization that I gave myself to do what I wished—and that Lacan supported. We do not talk much about the father's desire, which is nevertheless very important for a child.

MR: *Throughout your memoir—and also in your play* Goodbye Doctor—*you stress the importance of your relationship to language, especially to Portuguese, which you repeatedly brought into your free associations even though Lacan did not understand it. What is it about the native tongue that is so important to you? I admit that I ask this question as an immigrant who does not have the same relationship to my native tongue. Since my early twenties, my English has been better than my Finnish. I could never write a book in Finnish. Nor do I have any desire to do so. I am consequently intrigued by the intensity with which Portuguese appears in the analytic sessions and in your memoir as an object of yearning. Why do you think that this is the case?*

BM: I learned foreign languages at school. But all my training took place in Portuguese and in Brazil. Portuguese is the fifth most spoken language in the world. It is a very beautiful language that I have mastered better than any other. I cannot write fiction in French and I cannot do without Portuguese. Moreover, in my youth, I was very attached to my native country, like other Brazilians. At that time, no one left Brazil, which is in some respects a Dionysian country. This is significant. In addition, there are important countercultures and exceptional artists in Brazil. Unfortunately, it is also a very unequal country with largely oblivious elites. This is one of the reasons why I got married in France. My family is Franco-Brazilian, and I value this duality very much. France is a profoundly democratic country with a great cultural tradition and a keen sense of memory. Nothing is worse than forgetting since that is the source of repetition. This goes for subjective history and also for the history of the world, which inspires me in my novels.

MR: *Despite your obvious love of Brazil, you also had a seemingly conflicted relationship to the country when you were doing your analysis.*

On the one hand, you felt freer in Paris than you had in Brazil, especially as a woman. In Paris, you were able to do things, such as have lunch at a bar by yourself or walk the streets safely at night, that you were not able to do in Brazil. You also had an immense appreciation for the cultural, artistic, and architectural offerings of Paris. On the other hand, your longing to return to Brazil comes across clearly in both the memoir and the play. There are even moments when this longing is so strong that you almost interrupt your analysis. How do you account for your intense desire for a country that had in some ways wounded you and that held many painful memories, from the racism of having been called a "little Turk" to the romantic betrayal of your companion? If things were easier in Paris, why did Brazil draw you so powerfully?

BM: We are contradictory beings. "The heart has reasons that reasoning does not know." I love the language of Brazil, its fantasy, its landscapes, and I have organized myself to live a few months a year in the Atlantic forest, in Bahia, where I write under a sacred African tree, the *gameleira*. Brazil probably has some of the highest levels of violence and femicide in the world, but it is also a country where a gentleness and kindness are expressed in ways that I cannot find anywhere else. This is the case especially in Bahia, where Richard Ledes, who directed *Adieu Lacan*, went before making the film. This is also the place where Jorge Amado and the great musicians and performers of *bossa nova* and *tropicalia*—João Gilberto, Gilberto Gil, Caetano Veloso, Maria Bethania, and Gal Costa—emerged. They bravely resisted the dictatorship. Popular culture is the best thing about Brazil. I cannot do without it and I wrote two books about it, *Le Pays du Ballon Rond* and *Dans les coulisses du carnaval*. I wrote these texts when I returned to Brazil after my analysis because I realized that I had to listen to the performers and the carnival people. I discovered America thanks to Lacan, as he had told me I would—it was not just a joke.

MR: *One of the dilemmas you deal with in your analysis is the tension between the views that your family held about the traditional role of women and your own views as an independent, career-oriented woman. How did you end up navigating this tension in your life? Did it entail a rupture with your family? Or were you able to maintain a relationship with them while pursuing your own path? Did you feel that Lacan was nonjudgmental about the path you had chosen? He certainly did not seem to discourage you. Did he actively encourage you to follow "the truth of your desire" when it came to this issue?*

BM: I never broke from my family. I have written novels where I have spoken freely about the archaism of one's ancestors. When you write, you do not need to split off the past; you can simply ignore what is not worth the effort. This is a behavior that I have always adopted and that one can have when one has gone through an analysis and can access the symbolic and express oneself through it. One becomes a pacifist, so to speak. Among other things, Lacan taught me not to idealize power struggles. And he supported me when it came to motherhood. In my memoir, I recount the session where I told him that I could not have children because I could not remember the song my mother sang to me as a baby. His response was beautiful: "You'll invent another one!" He supported my desire to be a mother and at the same time, he emphasized reinvention. It is also thanks to this that in one of my books, *Carta ao filho*, which I presented at the Miami International Book Festival, I explain that the template for a perfect mother does not exist. Elisabeth Badinter, whom I had the pleasure of interviewing, says that the ideal mother is as rare as a Mozart.

MR: *The question of motherhood arose relatively late in the analysis. You link it to the desire of your father in the sense that there was something about your father's inability to "share" you with other men— his jealousy toward men with whom you might have sought an intimate relationship—that impeded your capacity to become a mother. Can you speak more about this dynamic with your father and about the resolution of the impasse in your analysis, which led to the possibility of you becoming a mother?*

BM: I think my desire to be a mother was less a reaction to my father's jealousy than to his desire for me to follow a career of consequence. In his own way, he was a feminist before his time. He woke me up every day with *mens sana in corpore sano* [a healthy mind in a healthy body] and supervised my swimming lessons, which I took very seriously. Additionally, I studied in an American school in São Paulo, the Graded School, while taking private French classes from the ages of five to eleven. My father wanted me to be a doctor like him, so I did what it took to become one. It is surely thanks to this relationship that I later had very good interactions with men and that I could not stand machismo, which is contrary to love, a theme that is dear to me. This probably explains why I married a Frenchman, who is no longer alive, and why the man I live with is also French. Machismo is one of the most serious problems that Brazil has to overcome. There are still judges for whom femicide may not be a crime. One cannot touch another's body against her will, nor can one justify rape by the victim's attitude. This is a thesis of Gisèle Halimi, one of the great French feminists. On the side of the feminist struggle, France can also be proud—beginning with the great book of Simone de Beauvoir, *The Second Sex*.

MR: *This is very interesting. I am glad that your father's attitude was not one of machismo. Did your choice of Lacan as your analyst have anything to do with your relationship with your father? How did transference work in this regard? Was Lacan able to help you to move from the desire of your father toward your own desire?*

BM: Yes, the choice of Lacan had to do with my father, who was also a great doctor and who wished for me to be one. He said that I had to enter the Faculty of Medicine through the narrowest door and to succeed in the most difficult competition. When he fell ill, I was in my second year of medical school, and he wanted me to take care of him so that I could learn to endure suffering and, perhaps, to prepare myself for his death. At the time, there was no escaping leukemia. Like my father, Lacan challenged me to succeed and he had all the authority I needed. He knew how to accompany his analysand as she needed to be accompanied, pushing her forward until she found her own way. I went to medical school, but I turned to psychoanalysis very early on and, thanks to Lacan, I founded a school in Brazil, the Colégio Freudiano do Rio de Janeiro, from where most of the Lacanian schools in the country originated.

MR: *I am terribly sorry about your father. Taking care of him must certainly have taught you about suffering and about death. It must have been an excruciating personal ordeal. Your memoir makes it sound like you were close to him. In contrast, your mother is a fairly conspicuous absence in your memoir. We know that she loved all things French and encouraged you to return to Paris after the collapse of your romantic relationship in Brazil. Beyond this, we do not know much about her. She seems largely excluded from the analytic work. Is this simply a function of the fact that you could not capture in your memoir all aspects of a four-year-long analysis? Or was she actually as absent in the analysis as she is in the memoir? If so, why is this?*

BM: My mother was as absent from my analysis as she was from my life during those years. This is perhaps because of her opposition to my sexual freedom, which was that of my generation. We must not forget that we were making the sexual revolution, saying *no* to the censorship imposed by society and by the family. This was only possible because of the pill. This revolution was necessary even if it resulted in a certain sexual tyranny: you had to have a relationship with somebody to prove that you were free; it was almost a categorical imperative. Today, the question is to have the subjective freedom to say *no* when you do not want to have a relationship.

I moved away from my mother to live my freedom, but since my marriage and the birth of my son, I grew closer to her and we both experienced reciprocal love again. I say *again* because during my early childhood we were very close. She inspired me to write two novels, *La Mère Eternelle* and *Hérésie*. She was a highly intelligent and human woman who knew how to gather people around her. She died at 103, perhaps to compensate for the early death of my father with whom she remained very much in love all her life. For years, having become almost blind, she had the letters they wrote to each other when they were engaged read to her every night. During her lifetime, she always made him present and knew how to transmit the delicate taste of love to us.

MR: *How lovely!*

You wrote the memoir more forty years after your analysis with Lacan. Why do you think it took you so long to do so?

BM: During a session, I told Lacan that I wanted to assess what had happened in my work with him. He answered me with a play on words, saying that I would make a Milan out of it—that is, that I would make a name for myself. I wanted to make a name for myself through my work as an analyst and a writer, and I had no intention of writing a memoir before the pandemic. I did not think it was necessary. During the lockdown, my partner insisted that I do it, and it was through writing that I discovered the value of it. It is always like that. I think through my writing. I could even say I write, therefore I am.

MR: *I can identify with that, as a writer. And I am very glad that you ended up writing the memoir. In it, you make it clear that you do not remember the details of all your sessions with Lacan. This would indeed be impossible for anyone after a forty-year hiatus. Was the distance of forty years an impediment in the writing of the memoir? Or did it help by allowing you to focus on the most important moments and turning points?*

BM: During my analysis, I took some notes that I kept for a long time. But they disappeared after I wrote *Perroquet de Lacan*, the novel on which I based my memoir and my analysis of the process followed by the Doctor. I obviously only talk about what was important: it is neither a journal nor a chronicle. I would like to add that in the novel, it is Seriema's story that structures the narrative—a story inspired by my own—and, in the memoir, it is Lacan in his profession, his function as an analyst, that constitutes the epicenter of the book. In other words, I told my story to shed light on his way of acting and not to talk about myself—perhaps precisely because this text was written forty years after my analysis. I can say that I was surprised by my own writing, probably as much as the reader of the book will be.

MR: *Now I fully understand what you mean when you say that your ego plays no part in the memoir.*

Generally speaking, how would you characterize the functioning of memory in a work such as yours? Was it important for you to capture accurately the events as they unfolded? Or where you more interested in conveying the "affective truth"—the emotional tone—of your experience with Lacan?

BM: It is from what you call the affective truth that the analyst and the writer work, each in their own way. It is this form of truth that allows for the analysand to move forward and for the reader's attention to be grasped, respectively. In order to reach it through writing, I exclude information that would draw my readers away from the story, since it would force them to carry out a parallel reflection. I believe in *Nachträglich*—in afterwardness [*après-coup*]—and what matters most to me is to intrigue the reader. But it is not the reader I am thinking about when I write; it is me. I discard anything that might hinder or slow me down, anything that prevents me from writing at my own pace.

MR: *Your memoir reads a bit like a thriller, keeping the reader at the edge of her seat to find out what happens next. Did you create this effect on purpose? As a writer, did you deliberately write the memoir as a piece that on some level mimics an Agatha Christie mystery that induces the reader to want to know the outcome?*

BM: No, I did not have a thriller in mind, but it may appear this way precisely because I wrote the testimony long after the analysis and after having written some thirty books—novels, essays, plays, heartfelt letters. There is hardly a genre that I have not practiced, and when I wrote this memoir, I believe that I had reached degree zero of narcissism.

MR: *Can you speak a little bit about the relationship between the memoir and the play? The play is obviously a fictionalized account. Yet it is also autobiographical. You scramble some of the details, so that, for instance, in the memoir you hallucinate a rat in your apartment building whereas in the play the hallucination takes place at Lacan's waiting room. However, the core concerns of the memoir—your Lebanese ancestry, xenophobia, the role of women, your father's desire, and your desire to become a mother—are portrayed fairly faithfully in the play, which ultimately focuses on the last of these topics. To what extent, then, would you say that the play is autobiographical?*

BM: Is there anything an author of fiction writes that is not influenced by their life experience? Even to imagine a character that has nothing to do with yourself, you draw on what you have experienced. This does not mean that you are not inventing things that you have never experienced. I would say that my play is autofiction, since beyond certain situational similarities, I attributed experiences to Seriema and to the Doctor that Lacan and I have not lived. This stages the analytic process in a more effective way. I wrote several versions of the play—as I always do—but before writing the final version, I worked with Robert McKee, the great American professor of storytelling who is also the author of *Story*. It was a valuable experience and I hope that my play will one day be staged in the United States. Richard Ledes, through a loose adaptation, has made a film of it that I like very much.

McKee helped me see that Seriema had issues with gender and he even suggested that there be a progression in the way she dresses in the staging. I did not bring this up with Richard, but it is noticeable that Seriema appears at the beginning of the film wearing pants and is quite stiff, while at the end she wears a light dress with great flexibility. In my memoir, I talk about my issues with gender. Fortunately, we can speak much more freely about such issues today.

MR: *You wrote the play several years before you wrote the memoir. Why do you think this is the case? Was it easier to give a fictionalized account of your analysis with Lacan than to write a memoir? Why?*

BM: No, it was always more difficult for me to write fiction. Writing *Perroquet de Lacan* took me five years, and it took me three years to come up with the final version of *Goodbye Doctor*. In contrast, I wrote the memoir in three months. Perhaps because I had already thought a lot about the subject, it was already developed, and I was no longer afraid of the reaction of the psychoanalytic milieu. Since my crossing of the Atlantic, I had proven myself.

MR: *In reading the play, I was struck by the sarcastic tone of the analysand, Seriema. In the stage directions, you often guide the actress to use such a tone. This felt different from the tone of the memoir, where sarcasm does not enter the picture. In the memoir, you are at times disappointed and wounded. You also sometimes feel angry or frustrated. But I do not get the same sense of sarcasm—or indignation—toward the analyst as I do in the play. Is this intentional? Is there an explanation for the divergence of tones?*

BM: Seriema is a sarcastic character. This is a personality trait of mine, but Seriema is not me, which should not be forgotten. Besides, I realize, through your question, that I cannot do without fiction since it allows me to express certain traits that are not always in conformity with customs. As Proust says, "A book is the product of an other self from the one we manifest in our habits, in our social life, and in our vices." This other self presupposes exile for its manifestation. I exile myself in literature to let a part of me live that I cannot reveal in society.

MR: *In the play, you vacillate between soliloquy and dialogue to give the audience access to what the analyst and analysand are thinking in addition to what they are saying to each other. This works very well. Especially interesting are the analyst's private thoughts: his frustrations and fears in relation to his mother's refusal of cancer treatments; his bafflement with some of Seriema's statements and actions; and his doubts about the direction of the analysis. You concretely portray the analyst as a fallible creature who "does not know"—who is just as human as the analysand is. During your analysis, how much did you wonder about what Lacan was thinking? He did not seem to reveal a lot during the sessions, fending off your attempts to provoke him. Did you stay mostly focused on what was going on in your own mind during and after the sessions? Or did you formulate hypotheses—fantasies—about what he might have been thinking? If so, what was the content of these hypotheses?*

BM: Of course, I was sometimes taken aback by a question, a remark, or a silence, but this was infrequent. To tell the truth, I paid much more attention to myself than to Lacan. I did not wonder about his approach towards me. I had enough else to work through for myself. At the end of my analysis, I noticed that he was very tired, and that pained me. But for me he was always the Analyst—with a capital A. When he kissed my hand at the Congress in Rome, I did not believe what I was experiencing. It was in a restaurant in Trastevere, where the Doctor had gone to lunch with several of his students after the conference. He behaved like a great actor who was completely in control of his game, and I was very sensitive to this theatrical dimension, at 5, rue de Lille as well as at this restaurant in Trastevere.

MR: *In Anglo-American circles—even among Lacanian theorists—one often hears it said that Lacan was an amazing theorist but not a great analyst. From your memoir, I get the sense that you do not agree. You seem to think that he was a wonderful analyst? Am I reading this correctly? If so, what made him a good analyst?*

BM: Lacan was a great clinician. And this is due to the fact that he was a great theorist. It is not at all contradictory. It is because he introduced the subject of the signifier as a notion into psychoanalytic theory and because he said that the unconscious is structured like a language that he turned practice upside down and that it became more effective. Naturally, he was the first to illustrate his theory. Those who criticize his practice do not know about it and do not want to know about it. The passion of ignorance is the worst of human passions.

MR: *What do you see as the major advantages and disadvantages of Lacanian clinical practice?*

BM: Lacan's practice encourages the analysand to listen to herself and to make an effort to understand her personal discourse; it teaches the analysand not to waste time, and this seems to be decisive. Lacan did not respond to the unconditional demand for love because he wanted to bring out the analysand's desire, but he was warm and he knew how to wait when it was necessary—and as long as necessary. In my play, the Doctor talks about this in one of his soliloquies. I must add that if Lacan's practice had not been effective, he would not have had so many analysands. But it must be recognized that he could sometimes bewilder his patients. If his discourse occupied all the space of his seminars, in his way of conducting an analysis he was laconic.

MR: *What, in your view, are the features of Lacanian clinical practice that most clearly distinguish it from other analytic schools? Do you believe that there are patients for whom the Lacanian approach may not be the right one? I am thinking in particular about analysands who possess very little ego strength and who may therefore need to cultivate this strength before they are able to start to dissolve their ego. There are factors—both structural and familial—that can crush a person's ego. As much as I appreciate Lacanian theory and practice, I have always* *thought that people whose egos have been ground to dust may be better off starting with another analytic model, such as a relational analysis. What are your thoughts on this?*

BM: Those who attended the presentations of patients at the Saint-Anne Hospital were able to see Lacan's extreme skill. He approached the patient exactly as he should have done, with great tact and sensitivity. In one of the soliloquies in my play, the Doctor says—or rather says to himself: "But it does no good to insist; forcing the issue only increases resistance … That's not why I'm here. Be patient, Doctor!" Lacan had an abundance of patience and at the same time he could interrupt the session with a cut to precipitate the analysis. I remember what happened when I came back from Brazil without telling him and I was very depressed. He did nothing to bolster my ego. He told me that he was not there to be my guarantor. In short, a slap in the face. Obviously, you cannot do that with everyone. But reinforcing the ego does not make things better. What is important is to bring the analysand to listen to herself. Psychoanalysis is simultaneously an art of patience and a kind of delicate balancing act [*une forme de grand écart*].

MR: *I myself have done two analyses, one relational and another more Lacanian (not strictly so, but with someone whose approach was loosely Lacanian, though she did not use the short session). I feel like these analyses changed my entire life, giving me access to the kind of life that I would not have been able to lead without them. I get the sense that you feel the same way about your analysis with Lacan? Would you say that it changed your life? If so, how?*

BM: Yes, without a doubt, my analysis with Lacan changed my life. I was able to accept my origins, which deep down I had always denied, and my feminine sexuality, which was unspoken. I was able to become a mother when motherhood seemed beyond my reach. That is to say, I became aware of myself in a completely different way. I talk about this earlier in this book and I explain how it became possible. Furthermore, I was able to confront my own death through fiction. When you believe in your death, you do not waste time—let us say that you waste less of it—and above all you live a better life. Death enlightens us; I see it as a guiding star. I know that Lacan did not want his life to be prolonged indefinitely and that he did not want to have surgery for his cancer. I spoke about this with Richard Ledes, who introduced this theme in *Adieu Lacan* with great deference.

MR: *I can relate to your commentary on death and not wasting one's time! Until recently, it felt that coming to terms with my own death was an impossible endeavor—one that always resulted in a pure abstraction. Now, for reasons that I will not go into, it is a concrete prospect, and you are right, the most noticeable difference is not wanting to waste any time! Time feels incredibly precious.*

Sometimes it feels that psychoanalytic clinical practice has a mysterious capacity to alter the analysand's destiny. To what do you attribute this effect?

BM: Remembering allows for an end to the trap of repetition and puts the subject in a position to reinvent their history. It is in this way that it can change destiny. But it takes a lot of know-how [*savoir-faire*] to bring the analysand to this end, to this tipping point. Lacan possessed this mastery, and it is this that I admire about him.

MR: *You yourself became a psychoanalyst. Did you take a strictly Lacanian approach? Or did you draw freely from different analytic schools? If the latter, which other thinkers besides Lacan influenced your clinical practice?*

BM: Freud and Lacan are my essential references. When it comes to a dream, I feel closer to Freud, who encouraged association. Otherwise, my sessions are variable-length. I use the cut, though differently from the Lacanian way. Sometimes I ask the analysand if it is okay with her to interrupt the session. Of course, the session can be short. But this is not a rule, and I do not try to imitate Lacan. Certainly not. He is inimitable.

MR: *What is the cut like from the perspective of the analyst? How do you determine when to cut the session? How do you know when the right moment is?*

BM: This is a fundamental question to which there is no ready-made answer. When it comes to the cut, it is intuition that guides me. I hear repetition in the analysand's discourse, the sudden discovery that recollection brings, the slip of the tongue, the change in the voice. I hear it and I make sure that the analysand hears it too. This can be done in different ways, for example by repeating the slip of the tongue that the analysand did not notice. Sometimes an analysand tells me that for her the session is over. For her, what had to be said has been said and that is the end of it. The analysis continues in the next session.

MR: *Along related lines, how do you, as an analyst, know when to offer an interpretation or to otherwise intervene in the analysand's discourse? This has always been enigmatic to me as a patient. Both of my analysts knew exactly when to insert their comments, which were usually short and opaque—designed to elicit my desire to keep analyzing on my own. When I asked them how they knew when to intervene, they merely told me that they had been trained to know. How does analytic training help you to determine the right moment?*

BM: I rarely interpret by attributing meaning to what was said. Experience has shown me that this is unwise. The analyst and the analysand do not have the same referents, neither to themselves nor to the world, and interpretation can be experienced as invasive. I can intervene, for example, by asking a question that guides the analysand toward a possible discovery. The fact that I have undergone an analysis has prepared me to distinguish the analysand's subjectivity from my own and to better listen. Listening requires training, like writing. Jean-Claude Carrière, the great French screenwriter, told me that at the beginning of his career he would spend entire afternoons with Jacques Tati on the terrace of a café, imagining scenes while people watching. To use one of his formulas, he was building up his imagination.

MR: *I understand what you say about interpretations. I have always experienced these as invasive. Fortunately, neither of my analysts offered interpretations per se. They simply left me with a question or a thought to mull over until the next session. For me, this worked well. I had tremendous respect for their ability to determine the right time to insert a question or a short observation.*

For you, what is the hardest thing about being a psychoanalyst?

BM: The hardest thing, I think, is to lose a patient and not know why. This happens mostly at the beginning of one's practice. Experience helps to prevent this from happening.

MR: *What is the most rewarding thing about being an analyst?*

BM: To see that someone whose future is compromised by the abandonment of their parents, rape, or AIDS can get through it thanks to analysis. This is to say that a person can reinvent their life.

MR: *Are there characteristics—personality traits, if you will—that you think help a person to be a good analyst? Are there traits that are strictly necessary, traits without which one cannot handle analytic work?*

BM: It seems to me that flexibility is very important. It is not enough to be intelligent and to have extensive knowledge of the theory: you have to be flexible. It is not possible to be rigid when working with human beings. This is true for the analyst and it is also true for the film-maker. At the same time, you must have authority without being authoritarian. It is a continuous learning process, and I like this quest; it allows me to remain modest. During a stay in China, I met one of the doctors of the Tibetan monastery in Labrang—a distant colleague. When I asked him how long he had studied medicine, he answered: "Thirty-five years … I am still learning medicine every day." I do the same with psychoanalysis.

There is no question of my retirement. I will work as an analyst and writer until the end.

MR: *Somehow I knew from working with you on this book that retirement is not on the agenda. This is why it did not even occur to me to ask about it!*

I have one more question about analytic technique. Being an analyst demands the ability to listen extremely closely. I imagine that it must be challenging to maintain one's attention for long periods of time and from one analysand to the next. How do you counter the fatigue that must ensue?

BM: Lacan worked from eight in the morning to eight in the evening. Sometimes, during his summer vacations, he would phone and ask me when I was coming to see him. I think that his ability to listen for such long periods had to do with the fact that the analyst listens with a floating attention. It is a way of listening that is less tiring. I can hold it without interruption for four or five hours. Then I do something else that may or may not have anything to do with psychoanalysis. It is important not to strain too much in any activity.

MR: *You have managed to combine a career as an analyst with a career as a writer. It seems to me that these two tasks require very different skillsets. How have you been able to negotiate the transitions from one task to another? Are they equally important to you? Or has one been more a labor of love than the other?*

BM: Psychoanalysis was the most important thing for me until I started writing *Le Perroquet de Lacan* at the age of forty-five, when I had to leave my teaching and my clinic in Brazil to go to France. I did so because my husband wanted our son to be raised in the country of Rabelais, Voltaire, and Proust, and I can appreciate this. Writing the novel was an unimaginable challenge for me. I knew how to write, but I had no training as a novelist. I had to acquire it. I took a creative writing course in Iowa and, in addition, I interviewed great intellectuals in France for the Brazilian press: Octavio Paz, Nathalie Sarraute, Jacques Derrida, later Gao Xingjian, Claudio Magris ... I did my training partly thanks to them, a bit like the Tibetan doctor ... I loved this work and, in Paris, I lived in an environment of writers. Now I write for myself, for the newspaper, and I consult. That is to say, I work a lot. I am lucky to have good health.

MR: *During your analysis with Lacan, you clearly appreciated Paris. What was it that you found most attractive? Do you feel that the city has retained its charm to this day?*

BM: In the 1970s, Paris was a true wonder: an extraordinary cultural atmosphere and a very beautiful and well-groomed city where I enjoyed great freedom as a woman. I wrote a book about Paris, *Paris Never Ends*, which was published in several languages, including Chinese. Cliff Landers was the translator of the book into English.

As for today, a lot has changed. Earlier I adored the city because I could walk around without worry. But it has become very difficult to simply stroll, to wander the streets like before. I discovered Paris when the pedestrian was the king. Today, he or she is a victim.

MR: *Do you have any advice for analysts-in-training?*

BM: Here again, there is no ready-made answer. I would say something different to everyone depending on their personal history.

MR: *How about those who are seeking to enter analysis? I often get this question from my students: how do you know that you have found the right analyst?*

BM: The choice of an analyst depends on the fundamental fantasy of each person. If the analysis functions and as long as it functions, one can say that one has found the right analyst.

MR: *But what about the opening stages? I find the many people have trouble determining whether the analyst that they have entered into analysis with is the right fit for them. Personally, I knew to stay away from analysts who offered interpretations too readily, sometimes even in the first session. It was an intuitive recoil on my part. Do you think that intuition is a good guide? Or is there a more rational way to know when the fit is not right?*

BM: Intuition is an excellent guide when choosing an analyst. However, I also think that one can make a mistake, and that it may sometimes be necessary to change analysts when one senses that one's analyst is abusing his power.

MR: *What would you say to your readers as your parting thoughts? Do you have any final words of wisdom?*

BM: I would simply say to close our interview that the ethics of psychoanalysis respects singularity and that only listening is the guarantor of peace.

ACKNOWLEDGMENTS

The completion of this work owes much credit to

- Cliff Landers and Chris Vanderwees, enthusiastic translators—
  the former of the play, the latter of the memoir and the
  interview;
- Richard Ledes, director of the film *Adieu Lacan*, who
  successfully mobilized his knowledge of psychoanalysis;
- Lois Oppenheim, who offered to send my memoir to my
  American publisher;
- Mari Ruti, whose unfailing support has accompanied me
  throughout this editorial adventure;
- Jean Sarzana, my daily companion, for his patience and
  complicity.

May they receive here my warmest and most sincere thanks.